About the author

Joseph Wandel is an assistant professor in the Department of Modern Languages at Loyola University, Chicago, teaching German language, literature, and culture. During his nineteen years at Loyola he has taught all of the German courses listed in the undergraduate bulletin but in recent years he has concentrated on the language courses. Educated at the University of Cologne, he took courses at the University of Wisconsin, Milwaukee, and then earned his M.A. from Marquette University and his Ph.D. from Northwestern University. Dr. Wandel is a member of the American Association of Teachers of German, the Literary Society of Chicago, and the German American National Congress.

The
German Dimension
of
American History

The
German Dimension
of
American History

Joseph Wandel

Nelson-Hall nh Chicago

Library of Congress Cataloging in Publication Data

Wandel, Joseph.
    The German dimension of American history.

    Bibliography: p.
    1. German Americans—History. I. Title.
E184.G3W35   973'.04'31   78-26050
ISBN 0-88229-147-5

Manufactured in the United States of America

10   9   8   7   6   5   4   3   2   1

Contents

Preface

There are innumerable individuals who came to the United States from Germany after World War II. Since their stories are too numerous to recount, I will tell my own story, as one example, and as an introduction which will perhaps aid in understanding why I wished to write this book.

When in 1948 the Berlin Airlift and the withdrawal of American troops in Korea gave rise to the political speculation that the Russians would be bold enough to take over all of Germany, I thought it high time to leave my home in Cologne. Having been a Prisoner of War in Russia for fifteen months and released from imprisonment only on the brink of starvation, I greatly feared being subjected again to Russian rule. I applied for an American visa with the support of my eldest brother, who had been living in the United States since 1927. The immigration quota was rapidly filled in those years, and I had to wait from 1948 until Christmas of 1951 to receive my permit. For me that visa was truly the best Christmas present possible.

Before I could leave for America, however, some personal matters had to be settled. I requested a release from a teaching contract at a German private high school, and was married on February 1, 1952. The following month I had to leave my bride behind in Germany, since she had not yet received her American visa. I still remember my uneasiness as I said farewell to my wife, sisters, relatives and to everything the Old Country stood for. I had very little money, and life in a strange, new land would be difficult. One of my brothers who accompanied me to the ship comforted me with an old German expression: "Keep your chin up even if your neck is dirty."

Dirty neck and all, I joined my eldest brother and his family ten days later in Milwaukee. With tears in his eyes he welcomed the "Benjamin" of our family of eleven. It was he who gave me a start in a country still strange to me, and taught me my first American saying, which is still the guiding motto of my life, "Go ahead, but take it easy!"

My practical and down-to-earth sister-in-law made the suggestion that I take a job in a factory after a few weeks of adjustment. With money earned on the assembly line, I paid for my wife's fare to America, and she joined me in September of 1952. I even saved enough money to pay the doctor bill for our first-born boy, who arrived on October 29, 1952. Along with my fatherly pride I also felt envy of that little rascal—who was an American citizen before I could be one. But I was on my way, and became a naturalized citizen in September 1957. However, I had not come to the United States to spend the rest of my life in a factory, and was anxious to get back into the teaching profession.

While working a nightshift in a factory to provide for my family, I continued my studies at the State Teachers College, Milwaukee (now the University of Wisconsin, Milwaukee), in the summer session of 1952. I obtained a teacher's certificate for secondary education in 1955 which allowed me to teach Latin, German, and English in high school. Twenty years earlier in my English classes at a German high school, I had learned "all beginnings are hard." Now the going was very rough indeed and the axiom became more than true. Things became even more complicated when my

wife became pregnant with our second child. With heavy
hearts we decided that my wife and first child should return
to her parents in Germany until my studies were half-way
over, and I had saved enough money to afford a move from
our two-room apartment to bigger quarters. We parted in
the fall of 1953, to be reunited twenty months later in 1955.
Our second son was born January 1, 1954, in Cologne,
Germany.

In 1955 I did not take a high school teaching position
but instead began work on my M.A. at Marquette University
in Milwaukee. Obviously, I had to keep my factory job. I
also taught German part time at Marquette as a graduate
assistant to meet the expenses of my growing family. On
Christmas Eve, 1957, our only girl was born; we were de-
lighted and felt the occasion was almost like a reward for
all the hard work and struggle we had experienced. The
next year brought me an M.A. and a job at Loyola University, Chicago, as in instructor of German. I furthered my
studies by earning a Ph.D. at Northwestern University,
Evanston, in 1965.

Thinking back on those years of establishing myself in
America, many memories, pleasant and unpleasant, come to
my mind. A German salesman doing business in several countries had told me, in 1953, that Germans were not welcome
in foreign countries.

Some of my fellow workers in the factory let me know
that I was not entirely welcome in the United States: "Why
did a 'superman' like you come here taking jobs away from
native Americans?" "Well," I answered, "you are the super-
men now and I am only a damn foreigner who, by the way,
entered this country legally and wants to become a teacher—
someone America needs." In spite of this and other argu-
ments, we remained—to my surprise—buddies, talking and
joking together, and having beers together on payday.

Other questions came from my teachers: "Why didn't
you openly oppose Hitler and denounce the atrocities committed by the Nazis?" "I did not vote for him," I answered,
"I was fifteen when he came to power." I also explained that

denouncing atrocities in a police state was not all that easy
unless someone wanted to become a "dead hero." I was
simply too young to become a martyr of a cause I did not
fully grasp. With the news media controlled by the Nazi
party, one learned about concentration camps only by
hearsay.

I became somewhat angered when people tried to tell
me that those atrocities were "typically German," or when
I read in an English dictionary under the entry *Hun*: "Asiatic
tribe; name for German soldiers in World War I and II." This
matter came up several times in my German classes, and I
told my students that, although the German soldiers had
not been angels, neither had the Russian and American
soldiers. "It is time," I added, "that we consider all these
crimes as being committed against fellow human beings and
not only against Jews, Indians, Vietnamese, or whatever
race or nation, and that we should all be equally ashamed of
them." The emergence of these awkward questions has not
affected the good relationship I have kept with my students.
They often stare at me in astonishment when I tell them
that I am glad that Germany lost the war. However, they
agree with me when I argue that being in America is certainly preferable to being a soldier in Siberia as part of
German occupation.

Americans could scarcely imagine how relieved I felt
that I could discuss such problems freely here in America
without being watched by a guard or Gestapo. A small,
rather insignificant story may express my pleasure in having come to a free country. Once, on my way to work I had
transferred to a second bus. The busdriver at the station was
waiting leisurely for the time of departure. "Well, Mack,"
remarked a fellow boarding the bus, "you are getting lazier
than the President!" I was astonished, but everyone smiled,
and no "Gestapo" came to arrest what would have been
considered a disloyal citizen in Nazi Germany.

When in 1958 I started my teaching career at Loyola
University in Chicago, my struggles, especially my financial
difficulties, were far from over. At first I was faced with the

dilemma that my starting salary was less than the one I had earned as a semiskilled worker in Milwaukee. That meant our family still had to economize, and would even more so, when I started studies for a Ph.D. at Northwestern University. At times I did not have the money to buy the textbooks for my courses and had to borrow them from a sympathetic professor. Moreover, our youngest child, our third son, joined the family on March 14, 1961, and wanted to be fed and clothed as well.

But by then I had become accustomed to the American way of life, summed up by a friend who claimed, "When I came to the United States I did not have a single penny; and now I'm twenty thousand dollars in the hole." Inspired by his experience I even dared to buy a house and car to share the predicament of millions of fellow Americans. Despite constant struggles, I am thankful for the privilege to teach my native language, as well as German literature and culture, to American students. I am convinced that my sacrifices will benefit my children, and that my struggles are small compared to those of the early German-American settlers, who came in much harder times to build a life of worth in their new country.

I want to express my gratitude to Dr. Anne M. Callahan, chairperson of the Modern Languages Department of Loyola University of Chicago, for encouraging me to write this book and to Loyola University for its grant which helped to cover part of my costs.

And particular thanks to my son, John W. Wandel, who brushed up my English and assisted in proofreading and typing the original drafts.

I am indebted to Barbara Clarke for helpful editorial suggestions.

Part 1

German-Americans
in
American Life

The German element represents the largest ethnic group in the population of the United States. One-fifth of our population, according to an estimate, has German blood in its veins. It is another interesting fact that the Germans are the most evenly distributed of any of the foreign ethnic groups. They settled in every one of the colonies and are represented in all states today.

Why and when did all those Germans come to the American continent? Religious persecutions, political situations and economic conditions in the home country prompted most Germans who came here to seek a better life for themselves and their children. In addition, there was probably a great deal of unrest or *Wanderlust* which drove scores of Germans as individuals or groups to America, even before England had established her colonial power.

Colonial America saw the first organized settlements of Germans in 1683. Most of those Germans were farmers and craftsmen, with the exceptions of their educated religious leaders and teachers. German immigrants from almost every province of Germany had settled in almost every Eastern colony at the beginning of the Revolutionary War. The distribution was estimated as follows:

New England	1,500
New York	25,000
Pennsylvania	110,000
New Jersey	15,000
Maryland and Delaware	20,500
Virginia and West Virginia	25,000
North Carolina	15,000
Georgia	5,000

Albert B. Faust, in *The German Element in the United States*, Volume 1, from which this estimate is taken, asserts:

This estimate is very conservative, being based upon estimates of the numbers in known German colonies. The number of scattered German settlers in the large cities, and the number of settlements of which there is no record, must have been quite large. An estimate of two hundred and twenty-five thousand inhabitants of German blood at the outbreak of the Revolution must therefore be regarded as a minimum. It would mean that a little more than one tenth of the total white population at the beginning of the War of Independence was of German blood. In certain localities, of course, the German population was much larger in proportion to the total population, notably in Pennsylvania, where it was one third of the total number. Future researchers in the colonial history of the Germans will undoubtedly reveal larger numbers than have been given above, but the attempt has been made here to confine the estimate within limits that are clearly incontestable.[1]

In the nineteenth century immigration from Germany surpassed that of any other ethnic group, totaling 5,009,280. Ireland follows with 3,871,253. This figure is relatively reliable, because after 1820 fairly accurate census reports of foreign immigrations were kept. The German immigration by decades was recorded as follows:

Decade	Immigration
1821-30	6,761
1831-40	152,454
1841-50	434,626

1851–60	951,667
1861–70	787,468
1871–80	718,182
1881–90	1,452,970
1891–1900	505,152

Perhaps the best characterization of this period of German immigration can be found in Faust's work. It is an abstract rather than a literal quotation of a treatise on the subject by Friedrich Muench,[2] a nineteenth century immigrant himself:

There were three periods. Immigration No. 1, attracted by such books as Duden's[3] turned to Missouri and other Western states, and devoted themselves to agriculture. Laborers and peasants, without any high standard of life and accustomed to hard work, found the situation to their satisfaction and gradually but steadily became prosperous. The better educated, sometimes even in spite of strenuous efforts, frequently died in the struggle. The adventurers of this group also met with disappointment, and, although frequently useful as border fighters on the advance guard of civilization, did not achieve permanent success. There was also a group of refugees of 1817–18, and it was their office to elevate the tone of the other German immigrants. The Germans were commonly all Jeffersonian Democrats in their politics, as distinct from the aristocratic Whigs, and they were opposed to slavery. After the Mexican War and the discovery of gold in California, conditions in the West grew better and the German farmers became more prosperous.

The immigration No. 2 was heartily welcomed by the first immigration, but the former were not well satisfied with their countrymen in America. They did not like the backwoods condition of the earlier immigration, and only a few of them, as did Hecker,[4] became farmers. Most of them went into the cities as merchants, manufacturers, or brain-workers of various kinds. A very frequent occupation for them was journalism, and in their newspapers they declared that we older men had not remained German enough, nor had we asserted our influence sufficiently. A war of words frequently occurred between the representa-

tives of the two immigrations, the older receiving the
nickname, "die Grauen," and the younger "die Gruenen."
The Grays had passed through an experience of twenty
years of toil under primitive American frontier conditions,
and had lost much of their youthful ardor for impractical
ideas. When the younger element, the Greens, arrived,
they set themselves up as instructors or dictators, but the
Grays were not disposed to listen to them. A better understanding came about when the new Republican party arose
and the Lincoln campaign began. Then the Germans
united against slavery as one man, and the old wounds
which the Grays and the Greens had inflicted in their
newspaper campaigns were entirely forgotten. The Greens
were useful in quickening the minds of the older generation; the latter, forming a conservative element, restrained
the new arrivals in their fantastic dreams. Without the
first immigration, the second would have had a much more
difficult position. It would not have gained influence and
would have made many a false step. Without the support
of the first immigration, the second might have been
quickly absorbed without leaving a trace behind. The
second played an important part in American history.

The third immigration came after the period of 1866.
They were mostly of the working class, with far better
schooling than the same class of thirty years before. In
comparison with the earlier immigrations they were over-
bearing, dissatisfied with conditions as they found them in
the new country, and too well impressed with those they
left at home. As a rule they would not do the work of an
inferior class, and as a result frequently found all desirable
positions occupied.

Even these [Faust says] as a rule prosper well. Conditions are so much better here than they were thirty or
forty years ago, and though the immigrants come in hundreds of thousands, they will find a place after paying for
their necessary experience. I have no fear for the green or
even the greenest [die Gruenen and Allergruensten].[5]

*Historical Statistics of the United States, Colonial Times
to 1957* gives the following figures of twentieth century immigration to the U. S. for the first five decades.

1910	2,311,085
1920	1,686,102
1930	1,608,814
1940	1,237,772
1950	984,331

There were two important groups of German immigrants in our century. The first group was composed mainly of German Jews who had to flee the persecution of Nazi Germany. Starting in 1933, about one hundred forty thousand German Jews came to the United States by the end of the decade. An estimated ten thousand of them were university educated. Generally, they belonged to the middle or upper middle class, and contributed immensely to the intellectual and economic wealth of their adopted country. German scientists and specialists made up the other important group, which arrived in the United States at the end of World War II. Although smaller in number than the first group they gained prestige by helping the United States to expand its space exploration efforts rapidly, and ultimately to land a man on the moon.

German immigration to the United States continues. Because of the economic rebirth of Germany which followed gradually after the disaster of World War II, the number of German immigrants in the last few decades is relatively small. Nevertheless, the *1970 U.S. Census of Population* lists the total German-born population as 3,622,035.

1
Early Arrivals

The first German ever to set foot on American soil was, according to the Norse sagas, a man named Tyrker, a member of Leif Ericson's expedition. As legend has it, Tyrker knew about vines and grapes, and found many along the northern coasts, which prompted Leif Ericson to name the New World "Wineland the Good."

Peter Minuit (Minnewit in German) was the first German to gain prominence in the New World. Peter was born in Wesel on the Rhine and arrived in New Amsterdam in May 1626. He was engaged by the Dutch government, and became the first governor of New Netherlands. It was he who purchased the island of Manhattan from the Indians for twenty-four dollars in gold. He then had a stone fort built on the tip of the island in case the Indians should change their minds. Thus, he encouraged increased European settlement on the island. He expanded the fur trade and protected it by ordering the construction of a thirty-gun warship, the *New Netherlands*. He later joined the colonial service of Sweden and became governor of the colony along the banks of the Delaware.

Other Germans also took important roles in the govern-

ment of the colony of New Sweden before it became a part
of New Netherlands in 1655. Its commissary was Hendrick
Huygen from Cleve on the Rhine. Another German, Peter
Hollender Ridder, governed the colony from 1640 to 1643,
and was succeeded by Johann Printz, a German nobleman
from Pomerania. The last head of the colony of New Sweden
was Heinrich von Elswich, a merchant from Luebeck. It is,
therefore, no surprise that German became the diplomatic
language used between New Sweden and New Amsterdam.

In 1664 England took over the Dutch colony on the Hudson, and New Amsterdam became New York—named after
the brother of Charles II, the Duke of York. The Dutch
landowners were allowed to retain their holdings. Trouble
started, however, when King James II combined the colonies
of New England, New York, and New Jersey, because the
Dutch population of New York feared to be overshadowed
by the neighboring Puritan colony. Their popular party was
opposed to the aristocratic Tory party and turned to Jacob
Leisler for leadership.

Born in Frankfurt on the Main, Leisler arrived in New
Amsterdam in 1660, as a soldier with the Dutch West India
Company. After his service he prospered as a trader and
ship-owner and later increased his fortunes by an aristo-
cartic marriage. One of his great-great-grandsons was Gou-
verneur Morris, member of the Continental Congress from
1777 to 1779.

When the Dutch rebelled against the dictates of James
II in 1689, Leisler became commander in chief of the colony.
He organized a militia to protect the colony against the invasion of French and Indian troops, and formed a council
of the governors of Massachusetts, Plymouth, East and West
Jersey, Pennsylvania, and Maryland. The council convened
in New York and decided to launch an expedition against
Quebec. Although its military mission proved a failure, the
council itself was later copied as a pattern for the first Continental Congress.

England regained control over the rebellious colony of
New York by the end of 1690, and Leisler and his son-in-law
Milborne were executed. In 1696 Leisler's family petitioned

the English Parliament and succeeded in restoring the property and civil rights of the family. Jacob Leisler, leader of the popular party, is historically the first American to oppose the aristocratic Tory element as a democrat and protagonist of the common man.

John Peter Zenger, destined to become a champion of the free press, arrived in New York in 1711 as a bond servant committed to work to repay his passage. For six years he served as an apprentice to the Royal Printer of the New York Colony, William Bradford. Later he opened his own printing shop which published the first arithmetic book in the colonies. In December of 1733 he began publishing the *New York Weekly Journal* in which he attacked the colonial government as corrupt and dishonest. He was charged with seditious libel and brought to trial on August 4, 1735. English Common Law considered any statement, whether true or false, as criminal when it scandalized an individual or institution; but the jury agreed that truth is the criterion in a libel suit. Since Zenger had published the truth, he was acquitted, and continued to publish the *Weekly Journal* until his death in 1746.

The German John Lederer was one of the early explorers of the New World. Born in Hamburg, he had come to Jamestown in 1668. Sir William Berkeley, governor of the colony of Virginia, sent him on three different expeditions during the year 1669-1670. He was supposed to find a passageway through the mountains of West Virginia to the Indian Ocean (which Governor Berkeley assumed to be west of the Appalachian Mountains). Lederer did not succeed in transgressing the several mountain ranges running parallel to the west. He concluded, however, that the then common belief that the continent of North America (lying between the Atlantic and Indian Oceans) could be travelled in eight or ten days was a great error.

From Lederer's map and journal, published in London in 1672, we learn that he went as far as the Santee River in South Carolina, where no white people were living at the time. According to the journal the first journey took Lederer from the head of the York River due west to the Appalachian

Mountains; on the second trip he went from the falls of the James River west and southwest into the Carolinas; finally he journeyed from the falls of the Rappahanock west to the mountains. Lederer's companions from Virginia had deserted him on his second trip and had returned to Virginia, where they spread incriminating rumors against Lederer. They infuriated the people of Virginia by telling them that they had to pay for Lederer's futile journeys. Lederer, therefore, returned to Maryland where Governor Talbot found him to be "a modest, ingenious person and a pretty scholar." Lederer vindicated himself against the accusations of his former companions, as Talbot says, "with so convincing reason and circumstance that removed all unfavorable impressions." Thus, he lived from 1671 as a citizen in Calver County, Maryland, subsequently receiving permission to engage in the fur business with the Indians he had discovered.

The earliest known German explorer was Peter Fabian, who came to America from Switzerland. He was a member of the English Carolina Company sent out in 1663 to explore the Carolinas. As the scientist of the party he recorded the distances by the standard of the German mile. His report about the Carolinas appeared in London in 1665.

Another Swiss-German explorer, Francis Louis Mitschel (or Michel), is mentioned in the earliest history of Carolina by John Lawson, London 1709. Mitschel had been sent by his home canton, Bern, to select suitable land for a Swiss settlement. During several years of discovery, he explored large areas among the mountain ranges of Virginia, Maryland, and Pennsylvania.

A German by the name of Hiens or Hans was among the members of the La Salle expedition in 1687. He revenged the murder of La Salle with another companion by killing Duhaut and Liotot. Hiens subsequently left the expedition that had vainly sought the delta of the Mississippi. He is considered to have been the first German to reach Texas.

These individual Germans arriving early in the New World were joined by a group of laborers and tradesmen in the company of Captain John Smith. He founded an English colony at Jamestown in 1607 and referred to his German followers as "those damned Dutch." Paradoxically, this curse implied a certain respect for the hard-working and independent "Dutch." Captain Smith comments in his *The True Travels,* "As for the hiring of the Poles and Dutchmen to make Pitch, Tar, Glasse, Milles and Soape ashes, when the country is replenished with people and necessaries, would have done well, but to send them and seventy more without victualls to work, was not so well advised nor considered as it should have beene." For most of the other settlers of Jamestown Captain Smith used harsh words, "Adventurers that never did know what a day's work was, except the Dutchmen and Poles and some dozen other. For all the rest were poore Gentlemen, Tradesmen, Servingmen, libertines, and such like, ten times more fit to spoyle a Commonwealth, than either to begin one or but help to maintain one."

Germany herself had lost her prestige as a seafaring nation with the decline of the Hanseatic League at the end of the Middle Ages, and was not in a position to compete with England, Holland, Spain, or France for major portions in the New World. Many more Germans arrived on the American continent in the service of the major colonial powers.

2
The Early Communities

Organized settlement in America by Germans began in 1683 with the arrival in Philadelphia of thirteen families of weavers belonging to the Mennonite sect. Following the invitation of their Quaker friend William Penn, they had fled the persecution they were suffering in their hometown of Krefeld, Germany. The *Concord* was the ship in which they crossed the ocean, and October 6, 1683, the date of their arrival in Philadelphia, marked the beginning of the history of German settlements in the United States.

Francis Daniel Pastorius, a well-educated lawyer, was the leader of this small group of Mennonites. He had sailed six weeks earlier from Deal, England. The thirteen families settled on a tract of land six miles north of Philadelphia which today still bears the original name of Germantown. These newcomers faced difficult first years in the new home. Yet, as Pastorius described in his diary, with "Christian endurance and indefatigable industry," Germantown soon became a thriving community of tradesmen, farmers, and gardeners. By 1689 the settlement was incorporated and Pastorius became its first mayor. In tribute to the industry of the townspeople, and in contempt of the vanity of mere book-learning, the new mayor remarked, "Never have metaphysics and Aristotelean logic . . . earned a loaf of bread."

Germantown was an extremely law-abiding community. To be sure, it had a tavern, but the townspeople were allowed to purchase only a quarter of a pint of rum or a quart of beer during a half-day, and there were hardly any arrests for drunkenness. The court which sat every three weeks frequently adjourned for lack of business. The court records do show, however, that a man named Mueller went to prison because he tried to smoke a hundred pipes of tobacco in one day on account of a bet; and one Caspar Karsten kept him company, because he had called the arresting officer a rogue.

It is perhaps surprising that the first formal protest against Negro slavery came out of this peaceful community. On February 18, 1688, a group of Germans met and formulated the document, which is in the handwriting of Pastorius. It was sent to the meeting of Quakers in Philadelphia, who avoided the complicated issue. Yet, Samuel W. Pennypacker, governor of Pennsylvania in 1906, said referring to the document, "A little rill there started which further became an immense torrent, and whenever hereafter men trace the causes which led to Shiloh, Gettysburg, and Appomatox, they will begin with the tender conscience of the linen-weavers and husband-men of Germantown."[1]

The constant struggle against Catholic France and Spain for dominion in the colonies naturally made England favor non-Catholic settlers. In keeping with this policy England furthered the immigration of the German Lutherans, the German Reformed, and the United Brethren (Moravians).

By about 1700, the number of Lutherans and Reformed was still relatively small in America, so that they often shared the same buildings for worship and sometimes even had the same minister. To further their own cause, the three Lutheran congregations of Philadelphia, New Hanover, and Providence united to ask the European authorities for a minister and contributions in money to build a church of their own. In 1741, Heinrich Melchior Muehlenberg was selected as pastor for the three Pennsylvania congregations. Having studied theology at Goettingen, he went to Halle where he prepared himself for his profession under the direction of the famed Pastor August Hermann Francke. After his arrival in America in the fall of 1741, he first paid a visit to Pastor Bolzius, the leader of the Salzburg colony in Georgia, to be prepared by him for the conditions awaiting a newly installed minister in the colonies. But when he heard that Count Zinzendorf, the spiritual leader of the United Brethren, had arrived in Philadelphia to try to unite the three different Christian denominations under one church roof, he hastened there to take firm possession of the office for which he had been contracted by the three Lutheran congregations.

For nearly fifty years Muehlenberg organized and led the affairs of the German Lutheran church in Philadelphia, becoming its revered patriarch. He settled many church disputes with tact and firmness, and kept friendly relations with the Lutheran Swedes, the Reformed church, and the Episcopalians. Bitter antagonism, however, existed between the Lutherans and the United Brethren during colonial times, each group claiming to represent the true doctrine of Luther. Due to Muehlenberg's untiring work the Lutherans soon exceeded the Reformed church in membership. St. Michael's Church in Philadelphia became too small, and in 1769 the famous Zion Church was consecrated to remain for years the largest church in Philadelphia. The memorial meeting in honor of Benjamin Franklin, who died in 1790, was held there under the auspices of the Philosophical Society in 1791. On December 26, 1799, Congress held its funeral services for George Washington in Zion Church, its walls ringing with Henry Lee's famous eulogy, "First in war, first in peace, first in the hearts of his countrymen."

The German Reformed church had a very competent leader and organizer in Michael Schlatter. Following the reforms instituted by Calvin and Zwingli, the German Reformed church is very close to the Presbyterians and the Dutch Reformed church in its religious doctrines. The Reformed Church of the Palatinate had also been requested by members of their faith in Pennsylvania to send ministers. Since the Palatinate church was poor and much persecuted, the Dutch Reformed church sent Schlatter, who arrived in Boston in September 1746, to be welcomed by the distinguished Dutch merchant, the Honorable I. Wendel, ancestor of Dr. Oliver Wendell Holmes. On his way from Boston to Philadelphia Schlatter summarized the impressions of his journey saying, "I can truly testify that often when contemplating the houses, the level country, the climate, and the sensible inhabitants, living in the same manner, enjoying the same culture, pursuing the same business, and differing but little from Europeans, I could scarcely realize that I was in a distant quarter of the world."[2]

Schlatter's report to the Dutch synods in 1751 was actually a cry for help. There were fifteen Reformed parishes with forty-six churches in the country, most of them without preachers or teachers. Given this situation, the proposal of a Scotchman, the Reverend Dr. William Smith, to teach the poor Germans not only sound Protestant faith but also sound government looked good to Schlatter, and he supported the idea. However, when the Rev. Smith suggested he could easily convert the Lutherans to the Episcopal church through these so called "charity schools," the Lutherans and Reformed hastily withdrew their support. Smith had also advised Parliament to deny political rights to immigrants for at least twenty years, showing clearly not only the religious but also the political motives for his charity school scheme. Smith failed, and Schlatter's popularity suffered so much by association that he resigned as preacher in Philadelphia and became army chaplain to the fourth battalion of the Royal American Regiment, which consisted mostly of Germans.

Both Muehlenberg and Schlatter were vigorous men of fighting spirit which had a great influence in leading eventually to armed resistance against the British oppression during the War of Independence.

The United Brethren were the most successful Christian missionaries among the Indians during colonial times. Yet their first missionary settlement, started in 1735 in Georgia, turned out to be a failure. When the Spaniards threatened Georgia, the Brethren were called upon to bear arms but refused because of their religious principles. They abandoned the settlement in Georgia and went to Pennsylvania, where they founded the towns of Bethlehem and Nazareth in 1741. Count Zinzendorf, their spiritual leader and protector when they had lived in Germany, visited them at that time. He stayed until 1743, leaving for Germany after an unsuccessful attempt to unite all Christian denominations of Pennsylvania. August Gottlieb Spangenberg became Zinsendorf's successor. Theological hatred had ousted Spangenberg from the professorship at the University of Halle, Germany. He worked as a cook for the ill-fated settlement of Georgia, and in Pennsylvania he did not mind working on the farm, confessing,

> As regards my outward occupation, it is at present farm work; but this is as much blessed to my soul as formerly my studying and writing. For nothing, even in outward affairs, is in itself good or bad, but whatever is done with the blessing of God thereby becomes good whilst anything performed without God's blessing becomes bad.[3]

From Bethlehem, Pennsylvania, the Brethren went out into the New York, Ohio and Michigan areas to Christianize the Indians. Christian Heinrich Rauch lived among the Mohicans in Schekomeko, New York, east of the Hudson, where he formed a small parish of Christian Indians. The white settlers were alarmed by his success. Rauch as well as two other missionaries, Buttner and Mack, were accused of being spies working for the French. The colonial authorities became suspicious, forcing the missionaries and their Indian flock to leave. They went to a part of the Western Reserve, now in Ohio, where they founded the Christian Indian village of Gnadenhuetton in 1746. Under the guidance of the Brethren the Christianized Delaware Indians became farmers. A church was built, along with two schools—one for boys and one for girls—because the Brethren did not believe in coeducation. Gnadenhuetton had five hundred inhabitants by 1749. Besides Gnadenhuetton two other Christian Indian villages, Salem and Lichtenau, were founded in the fertile valley of the Muskingum River. Another, Schoenbrunn, was built farther north, where the missionary David Zeisberger settled with the Delawares.

In 1781, Zeisberger, many Indian converts and other missionaries were forced to Michigan as hostages of the Wyandot and British. Some were allowed to return and were massacred at Gnadenhuetton by Americans under Williamson. Zeisberger returned later to the Muskingum and founded the Indian village Goshen. He died in Goshen in 1808, when he was eighty-seven years old. He had spent sixty years of his life with the Indians. Zeisberger and the missionary John Heckewelder (of German parentage) composed textbooks and dictionaries in the languages of the Onondagas, Delawares, and Mohicans. Today, Gnadenhuetton, Schoenbrunn, and Goshen bear monuments to Zeisberger and the Moravian missionaries.

Pennsylvania remained the center and stronghold of German settlement throughout colonial times. The German settlers of Pennsylvania were treated fairly by the authorities and prospered on the fertile land they had chosen and bought. Reasons for the success of the Pennsylvania Germans may be found in a booklet by Dr. Benjamin Rush, one of the signers of the Declaration of Independence and a noted Philadelphia physician. In "An Account of the Manners of the German Inhabitants of Pennsylvania, Written in 1789," Dr. Rush recorded the following:

> Germans produced in their children not only the *habits* of labor but a *love* of it. When a young man asks the consent of his father to marry the girl of his choice, he does not inquire so much whether she be rich or poor, whether she possesses any personal or mental accomplishments, but whether she be industrious, and acquainted with the duties of a good housewife.[4]

The Germans coming primarily from the Palatinate and settling in New York Colony were not as fortunate as their Pennsylvania compatriots. When the War of the Spanish Succession in 1707 devastated a portion of the Palatinate, the impoverished inhabitants sought the helping hand of "Good Queen Anne" of England. By October of 1709, thirteen thousand displaced Palatines were in London. Several American Indian chiefs on a visit to London took pity on the homeless and half-starved immigrants and offered a tract of land on the Schoharie River, in New York Colony, to settle the exiled Germans. Ten ships with three thousand Palatines sailed in April 1710, accompanied by Colonel Robert Hunter, the appointed governor of New York Colony, Nearly eight hundred did not survive the trip, and even the survivors were not settled in Schoharie, but on the eastern shore of the Hudson, where they set to producing tar and pitch for the English navy. When the production of tar and pitch did not come close to the expected yield, the Lords of Trade in London abandoned the project of establishing naval stores on the Hudson.

Governor Hunter's means to support the enterprise were also exhausted, yet he still demanded the Palatines to stay by in case work would be resumed. With no provisions and winter approaching, the Palatines decided to send a group of their leaders to Schoharie to ask the Indians for land. John Conrad Weiser and Captain Kneiskern were among this group, which received the promise of land and help from the Indians.

In a short time about fifty families made their way through the trackless forest from Schenectady to Schoharie Valley in spite of the governor's order "not to goe upon the land and he who did so should be declared a Rebell."[5] Instead, the Palatines "seriously weighed matters amongst themselves and finding no likelihood of subsisting elsewhere . . . found themselves under the fatall necessity of disregarding the governor's resentment, that being to all more eligible than starving."[6] They almost starved, and survived only because the Indians showed them where to find edible roots.

In March 1713, more Palatines moved to Schoharie, increasing the number of settlers to almost seven hundred. On both sides of the Schoharie River they founded seven villages named for their leaders: Weiserdorf, Hartmannsdorf, Brunnendorf, Schmidtsdorf, Fuchsdorf, Gerlachsdorf, and Kneiskerndorf. These settlements lacked almost everything to start farming. There was not a horse, a cow, nor a wheelbarrow; the settlers had to carry their belongings on their backs. Sickles served as ploughs, and in Indian fashion they ground

corn in stone mills. Salt and seed wheat were brought on foot
from Schenectady nineteen miles away. The harvest that
year was plentiful, with an eighty-five-fold yield of wheat.
Yet, for a generation these pioneers were compelled to carry
their grain on their backs to Schenectady to have it ground,
having no mill of their own.

In addition to the hardships, these settlers were harassed by the government, which three times granted away
from them the land they had bought from the Indians. At
first the Palatines offered passive resistance, simply staying
upon their lands. But, finally, they rebelled, driving out the
Albany sheriff who tried to eject them. This warfare with
the government went on for five years, when the Palatines
decided to send representatives to London to make an appeal for their rights. Conrad Weiser and two companions
arrived penniless in London, because they had been beaten
and robbed by pirates on their way.

In London the three were thrown into debtor's prison.
Released from prison after almost a year with a check of
about seventy pounds sent by their friends in Schoharie,
Weiser alone stayed five more years in London pleading the
cause of his countrymen. But his plea was unsuccessful, because the testimony of Governor Hunter, who had been recalled to London, weighed heavily against Weiser. On his
return to Schoharie, he advised his people to leave the colony
of New York for Pennsylvania. However, about three hundred remained in Schoharie, buying their land again on term
payments from the new landlords. They were joined later by
other settlers, so that by the time of the Revolution, the entire Schoharie country was settled. The farms of the German
settlers even extended twenty-five to thirty miles beyond the
original seven villages. After the turmoil of the frontier
struggles and of the Revolution, in which they actively took
part, they lived a quiet life. William C. Bouck, a descendant
of these hard-tried but successful settlers, became prominent
in politics and served the state of New York as governor,
1843 to 1845.

Governor Burnet treated the people of Schoharie better than had his predecessor Hunter, and offered them good
lands on the Mohawk River. Some of the Schoharie people
accepted the governor's offer and settled, under their leader

Gerlach, on both sides of the Mohawk. At this frontier post they protected the colony throughout the French and Indian War and Revolutionary War. By about 1750, the Palatines of the Mohawk Valley numbered from twenty-five hundred to three thousand. General Herkimer, the hero of the battle of Oriskany, became the most famous of the Palatines of Mohawk Valley.

About two-thirds of the Schoharie people set out for Pennsylvania. They were unwilling to buy their land again or be settled at the governor's pleasure on the Mohawk. This migration was made in two waves; the first beginning in the spring of 1723 and the second in 1728. With the help of their Indian friends they cut a road through the forests from Schoharie to the head-waters of the Susquehanna. From there, the women and children drove down the river, while the men guided the cattle along the banks. When they reached the mouth of the Tulpehocken they settled there. Their long journey from the Palatinate to London, and from there to the camps on the Hudson, to Schoharie, finally ended happily at the Tulpehocken. Johann Conrad Weiser and his son Conrad had remained in the New York colony. As a boy, and with his father's consent, Conrad had spent some time with the Mohawk Indians to learn the Indian language and customs. This experience proved to be very valuable later when Conrad Weiser became the official interpreter and mediator between the Indians and the colony of Pennsylvania.

The Germans of German Valley, New Jersey, were prominent farmers like most early German settlers. One of them by the name of Fuchs improved agriculture by introducing a new and superior variety of wheat. Farmers travelled to Foxenburgh from far away to buy wheat from him. Contrary to popular belief, the German farmers of New Jersey were not stingy. In 1760 they gave the sum of one thousand pounds, quite large for that time, for the support of the church and school of New Germantown. During the Revolutionary War, Pastor Nevelling of the Amwell Church mortgaged his property and loaned five thousand pounds to the Continental Congress, a sum he never recovered, having lost the loan certificate. He was one of several other German patriot pastors on whose heads the British had set a price. The grandson of another pastor, General Frederick Frelinghuysen distinguished himself in the battles of Trenton and Monmouth Courthouse. He later was a member of the Continental Congress Convention of 1787, and from 1793 to 1796 served in the United States Senate. Frelinghuysen is a distinguished German-American family name even today.

The New Jersey Germans kept their German speech and customs for a long time. As time went by, however, adjustments had to be made concerning even the religious service. The Reverend Caspar Wack, pastor of the Great Swamp Church, tried, from 1771 on, to preach in English to please the younger generation. An English officer listened to Mr. Wack's English sermon, and, thinking it to be delivered in German, remarked, "I never knew before that German was so much like English; I could understand a great deal of it."[7] Reverend Wack's English improved gradually. He took great pain to mark his manuscripts with the dictionary's pronunciation, though he never completely overcame his German accent. He also busied himself with farming from dawn to dark and operated a mill, becoming a wealthy member of the community. Musically inclined, he even found time to teach a singing school. Caspar Wack eventually moved to Stone Arabia in the Mohawk Valley, and he later served as a chaplain during the War of 1812.

Until 1807 the United Brethren managed the Hope Settlement in Warren County, New Jersey. William Ellery and William Whipple, two signers of the Declaration of Independence, mention this colony favorably in their diaries of 1777, "the strong, neat, and compact Moravian houses, mostly of stone, the mechanics' shops, the stores, and above all a mill, one of the finest and most curious mills in America."[8] The same mill is described by Chevalier de Chastellux, a French soldier of Lafayette's staff, who saw the mill in 1788:

Mr. Colver treated us with an anxiety and respect more German than American, and let us first to see the saw-

mill which is the most beautiful and best contrived I ever
saw. A single man only is necessary to direct the work; the
same wheels which keep the saw in motion serve also to
convey the trunks of the trees from the spot where they
are deposited to the workhouse, a distance of twenty-five
or thirty toises (making a total distance of over one hundred and fifty feet): they are placed on a sledge, which
sliding in a groove, is drawn by a rope, which rolls and
unrolls on the axis of the wheel itself.[9]

Augustin Herman was most distinguished among the
early settlers of Maryland. Born in Prague to Protestant
parents, he fought for a while on the side of King Gustavus
Adolphus of Sweden during the Thirty Years' War, but left
before that war ended. He arrived in Virginia about 1630
and from there he moved to New Amsterdam, where he became a prosperous tobacco merchant. He also served the
Dutch colony under Governor Stuyvesant on various diplomatic missions. The beauty of Maryland attracted him so
much that he offered to Lord Baltimore to make an exact
map of Maryland for the ownership of a certain piece of
land. Lord Baltimore accepted, because he needed the map
to settle boundary disputes with Virginia. The map Herman
drew received high praise not only from the Maryand authorities but also from the King of England, who called it
the best map he had ever seen. Herman received five thousand acres along the Elk River. He expanded his possessions
by fifteen thousand acres on which he founded Bohemia
Manor, St. Augustine Manor, Little Bohemia Manor, and
the Three Bohemian Sisters which formed the beginnings
of Cecil County. He also represented Baltimore in the
General Assembly.

Enterprising Germans from Pennsylvania helped greatly
in the settlement and commercial development of Baltimore
from its very beginning in 1730. A mill was built by G. M.
Meyer. The first brewery was established by D. Barnetz and
Leonard. Andrew Steiger was the first butcher of Baltimore,
acquiring large tracts of land in East Baltimore to feed his
cattle. This part of East Baltimore was known as Steiger's
Meadow. The first German church was built in 1758; a

second one in 1764. Both were Protestant churches. The
German Catholics were not numerous enough at that time
to afford a church of their own, and some preferred to join
the prominent English Catholic parishes.

Baltimore's first city council had three German alder-
men among its seven members. One of the three, George
Lindenberger, had founded a fire company and had been
a militia officer during the Revolutionary War. At the time
of the Revolution Baltimore already had a large German
population, which could afford to send several volunteer
companies to the aid of the patriot army. "The Baltimore
German," Jake Keeport (Kuhbord), was Washington's pur-
chasing agent. When the Continental Congress had to flee
Philadelphia, its meetings were held in Baltimore in a hall
owned by the German merchant, Veit. Many German families of Baltimore engaged in the tobacco trade, shipbuilding,
leather manufacture, and foreign trade.

The Pennsylvania Germans were just as important in
the settlement and development of western Maryland. From
Lancaster County they travelled south by way of an old
Indian trail they had widened. The first group arrived about
1729 and settled near the Monocacy River. Between 1760
and 1770 this Monocacy settlement was absorbed by Crea-
gerstown, a settlement founded by a German named either
Cramer or Creager. The Pennsylvania Germans had been
persuaded to come to Maryland by a very generous offer
made by Charles, Lord Baltimore, in 1732. At the rental of
one cent an acre families could secure two hundred acres;
single persons between the age of fifteen and thirty, one
hundred acres, with no rent to be paid for the first three
years. Thus, the modern day counties of Washington and
Frederick were settled largely by Germans.

Immigrants from Germany continued to arrive in Maryland. Prominent among those settlers was John Frederick
Amelung, who arrived from Bremen in 1784 and constructed
a factory for the manufacture of glass. President Washington
refers to it in a letter to Jefferson: "A factory of glass is
established upon a large scale on Monocacy River near Frederick in Maryland. I am informed it will produce this year

glass of various kinds to the amount of ten thousand pounds."[10] Amelung wished personally to contribute to the president "two capacious goblets made of flint glass, exhibiting the General's coat of arms." To make the presentation Amelung had come in full court costume. When he was met by a Washington in shirt-sleeves standing on a ladder to fix the grape vines, he almost dropped his precious gift, or so the story goes.

Middleton, Sharpsburg, Taneytown, Tom's Creek, Point Creek, Owen's Creek, Union Bridge, Emmetsburg, Woodsboro, Hauvers, and Mechanicstown are some of the many German settlements in western Maryland. West of the Blue Ridge two German settlements are worth mentioning, Conigocheague and Hagerstown. Hagerstown became the county seat. Its founder, Jonathan Hager, was elected by his district to the Assembly of Maryland. But before he could take his seat a new law had to be passed for him, representing the cause of naturalized citizens, since Hager had at first been declared ineligible. He was re-elected and placed on several committees.

Muehlenberg, a Lutheran patriarch, and Schlatter, a leader of the Reformed, organized many congregations and supplied them with ministers. Michael Schlatter comments on the "purity" of the German settlements in Maryland, meaning thereby the absence of sectarians. Besides the Lutheran and Reformed, there was only one other denomination in Maryland—the United Brethren. Between 1745 and 1747 they founded the settlement of Graceham, which remained for a long time a center of religious worship.

The Germans of western Maryland were mainly farmers. Their farms formed the link in the chain of German farms from Pennsylvania to the Valley of Virginia. Alexander Spotswood was governor of Virginia from 1710 to 1723. In April of 1714, he employed twelve German families who arrived from Westphalia, Germany, to establish and operate iron works for him. These iron works were built about ten miles northwest of the present town of Fredericksburg in Orange County. Initial success prompted the arrival of twenty more families in 1717, and forty families between 1717

and 1720. They settled at Germanna, a town the governor
had built for them. Although those Germans were skilled
iron-workers, the mining operations did not continue for
long. It seems that the governor and the miners got into a
dispute about who was owing money to whom. By 1748 all
but three German families had left Germanna.

Those who left established two settlements on the Pied-
mont Plateau, Germantown in 1721 and Little Fork in 1724.
The settlers belonged to the Reformed church and built
churches and schoolhouses. Since they could not afford
ministers right away, the missionaries of the United Brethren
found a friendly welcome. The people of the Reformed
church did not mind listening to the sermon of a Moravian
missionary, for, as brother Gottschalk comments, "the people did not look so much upon religion, but rather that Christ
be preached to them."[11]

The German Lutherans who left Germanna settled in
Madison County, Virginia. They became prosperous and
numerous and in 1740 built Hebron Church, one of the oldest
churches in Virginia.

The beautiful Valley of Virginia, situated between the
two mountain ranges of the Alleghanies and the Blue Ridge,
was densely populated by Pennsylvania Germans. They arrived as early as 1726, and by the end of the century the
German settlers were quite numerous. Historic Harper's
Ferry, where abolitionist John Brown was captured, was
founded by Robert Harper in 1734. Winchester, the capital
of Frederick County, had a mixed population of mostly Germans and Irish, with a few Scotch and English. This caused
some friction in the beginning. Samuel Kercheval, the historian of the Valley of Virginia, reports:

> It was customary for the Dutch on St. Patrick's Day to
> exhibit the effigy of the saint, with a string of Irish pota-
> toes around his neck, and his wife Sheely, with her apron
> loaded also with potatoes. This was always followed by a
> riot. The Irish resented the indignity to their saint and his
> holy spouse, and a battle followed. On St. Michael's Day
> the Irish would retort, and exhibit the saint with a rope
> of sauerkraut about the neck. Then the Dutch, like the

Yankees, "felt chock full of fight," and at it they went, pell-
mell, and many a black eye, bloody nose, and broken head
was the result. The practice was finally put down by the
rigor with which the courts of justice punished the
rioters.[12]

In the course of time, however, the Dutch and the Irish
accepted each other and frequently intermarried.[13] The
scattered German settlers who located near almost every
town of Virginia helped to make the state one of the richest
farming communities of pre-Revolutionary times. By settling on the western frontier they not only protected it but
also were ready for the move further westward, when the
time for it came.

In North Carolina the first German settlement was
New Bern. About six hundred and fifty Palatines under the
leadership of Cristoph de Graffenried and Louis Michel (also
spelled Mitchell), two German-Swiss, arrived in December
of 1710 at the confluence of the Neuse and Trent rivers. Only
a few months later, the settlement of New Bern suffered a
setback. In 1711, an Indian war broke out. The Tuscarora
Indians, with whom the white settlers had lived on friendly
terms, suddenly turned against them. Sixty or more people
around New Bern were killed. De Graffenried was captured
by the Indians and escaped torture and death by declaring
himself "King of the Palatines." Lawson, the surveyor-gen-
eral, was captured with de Graffenried and tortured. Land
surveyors were never spared by the Indians since they were
considered the cause of the land robberies. In a war of revenge, the Indians were either killed or removed to other
parts, so that by 1743 the settlers had spread all over what
is now Craven County.

The interior of North Carolina was settled by Germans
from Pennsylvania, who went overland through the Valley
of Virginia, their belongings packed in Conestoga wagons.
The first of these pioneers moved in 1745, and many more
made the trip in 1750. Land in Pennsylvania had become
more and more expensive, and members of large German
families looked for less expensive land in North Carolina.

Records in Pennsylvania counties show many family names
that can also be found in counties of North Carolina. The
Reverend Gotthardt Dellmann Bernheim, historian of the
early German settlements in North and South Carolina,
wrote:

> Had a traveller from Pennsylvania visited about forty or
> fifty years ago (1820-1830), portions of the present coun-
> ties of Alamance, Guilford, Davidson, Rowan, Vabarrus,
> Stanly, Iredell, Catawba, Lincoln, and some others in the
> State of North Carolina, he might have believed himself
> to have unexpectedly come upon some part of the old Key-
> stone State.[14]

The United Brethren purchased one hundred thousand
acres of land from Lord Granville, president of the Privy
Council of the government of Great Britain. The deed for
the "Wachovia Tract" in Forsyth County, North Carolina,
was signed on August 7, 1753. In October 1753, twelve single
brethren from Bethlehem, Pennsylvania, arrived there, and
named the new settlement Bethabara, "house of passing."
Among the twelve were a doctor and a tailor whose services
were more than welcome to neighboring settlers. The brethren soon built a mill to which people came from many miles
away to have their grain ground. When the Indian wars
came, Bethabara was fortified and became a refuge for many
who came even as far as from Virginia. Bethabara also welcomed and fed the Indians and became known among them
as the "Dutch Fort, where there are good people and much
bread."[15]

Spangenberg, the indefatigable bishop of the United
Brethren, founded the town of Bethany at a site three miles
north of Bethabara. For some time he and a few brethren
rode daily from Bethabara to the new settlement of Bethany,
a dangerous undertaking during the Indian wars. As the
Indians later confessed, they had often attempted to ambush
the cavalcade, but could not succeed, "for the Dutchers had
big, fat horses, and rode like the devil."[16] In 1766 the United
Brethren started to build their main settlement of Salem,

North Carolina, which is still today the center of the Moravian denomination in the South.

A number of little settlements grew around Salem. One of them was Friedland, meant to become a haven of peace for the much-tried emigrants from Broad Bay, Maine, who were led there by the Moravian brother Soelle in 1769. The United Brethren, known for their excellent schools, founded in 1804 the Salem Female Academy which has educated the daughters of many prominent families of North and South Carolina and other Southern states.

The first settlement in South Carolina was Purysburg. Its founder, John Peter Pury, had persuaded three hundred and seventy Swiss countrymen to settle in Purysburg during 1732:

> A man who shall have a little land in Carolina and who is not willing to work above two or three hours a day, may very easily live there. If you travel into the country, you will see stately buildings, noble Castles, and an infinite number of all sorts of Cattle.... The people of the Palatinate, those of New York, New England, and other parts sell all they have to come to Carolina.[17]

For a time, Purysburg prospered, in part due to its silk manufacture, an industry which Germans introduced to America. Pastor Bolzius on his way to Georgia remarked in his journal (May 1734) concerning Purysburg:

> This town is built on the more elevated banks of the river, and has many wealthy people residing here; it is hoped in a short time it will become a considerable town. The inhabitants labor industriously in their gardens and fields, and persons can already procure here fresh meats, eggs, garden vegetables, even more than in Savannah. We were shown all kindness, and several of the inhabitants besought us to return soon again, and administer the communion.[18]

In spite of these hopeful beginnings, Purysburg was gradually deserted by the German settlers who were forced to leave the malaria infested coast line for the healthier highlands in the center of the province. This westward movement had already started by 1735. The settlements originated in the present Orangeburg and Lexington counties, spreading from there to both sides of the Edisto and Congaree rivers into the neighboring counties such as Barnwell and Newberry. These German settlements were as far west as any other.

The settlement of Georgia began in 1732 after King George II of England had empowered a number of gentlemen to colonize the southern part of the Carolinas. General James Edward Oglethorpe founded the town of Savannah in 1733 by establishing a first group of English colonists. In 1734 they were followed by a group of German Protestants, the so-called Salzburgers, driven out of their homes in the Tyrolian Mountains by a decree of Leopold, Count of Firmian, Archbishop of Salzburg. They selected a piece of land about twenty-five miles southwest of Savannah, and "after singing a psalm set up a rock which they found upon the spot, and in the spirit of the pious Samuel named the place Ebenezer (the stone of help) for 'hitherto hath the Lord helped us.' "[19]

When in 1736 more Salzburgers arrived, Ebenezer was found to be an undesirable site for a colony. With the permission of General Oglethorpe, they chose a high ridge eight miles away where they established a town, which in a spirit of hope they named New Ebenezer. The new town prospered under the leadership of the pastors Bolzius and Gronau. Among other things, they produced silk and were able to send to England, in the year 1751, a thousand pounds of cocoons and seventy-four pounds, two ounces of raw silk. Thomas Jones describes New Ebenezer in a letter dated Savannah, 1740:

> The people live in the greatest harmony with their ministers and with one another, as one family. They have no drunken, idle or profligate people among them, but are industrious, and many have grown wealthy. Their industry has been blessed with remarkable and uncommon success, to the envy of their neighbors, having great plenty of all the necessary conveniences for life (except clothing)

within themselves; and supply this town (Savannah) with
bread-kind, as also beef, veal, pork, poultry, etc.[20]

Germans from New Ebenezer soon spread out and settled in other parts of the state. German farms were located
on the road leading from Savannah to Augusta and on the
banks of the Savannah River as well as on Lockner, Ebenezer, and Mill creeks.

New England had but a few early German settlements.
The first organized attempt to settle Germans in New England was made in the 1740s by Samuel Waldo. Like his
father Jonathon, Samuel was a wealthy businessman and
had acquired a tract of land in Maine. He appointed Sebastian
Zauberbuehler his agent to find Germans willing to emigrate.
Sebastian established himself at the inn of the "Golden Lion"
in the old Palatinate city of Speyer. He issued a circular de-
scribing in glowing colors the charms and fertility of the
coast of Maine. The prospective settlers were promised land,
the support of a minister and schoolmaster for ten years,
good food on the voyage, and a church. In addition, Waldo
promised to support the colonists for a year after their
arrival.

About three hundred people from the Palatinate and
the province of Wuerttemberg were persuaded to follow
Zauberbuhler to the promised land. Since no ship was available, they were detained for two months at Cologne. They
were not allowed to enter Holland, lest Waldo's Rotterdam
agents were obliged by contract to support them. After
having exhausted their own means, some of them went back
home, others diverted their emigration to Pennsylvania, and
many of the young men enlisted.

The remaining one hundred fifty to one hundred sixty
Germans finally crossed the Atlantic in August of 1742.
They received a warm welcome at Boston by Massachusetts'
Governor Shirley and by Waldo, who accompanied his col-
onists to Broad Bay. For the winter, however, he left them at
Waldoboro without the promised shelter, without clothing,
mills to make flour, or ovens to bake bread. The new German
colonists had to subsist during that first winter mainly on

broth made from rye, bruised between stones. Their minister left them. His place was filled by the schoolmaster John Ulmer who became their magistrate, prince, and priest. During the siege of Louisburg, Nova Scotia, he also became their military commander. The German settlers from Broad Bay who participated in this military campaign against France took their families along to Nova Scotia. The few who remained were attacked by Canadian Indians and either killed or taken into captivity.

After the peace of Aix-la-Chapelle in 1748, John Ulmer returned to Waldoboro with a few settlers. Waldo himself gave new life to the settlement bearing his name by bringing some twenty or thirty new families of Germans from Philadelphia. The primitive huts gave way to decent houses, mills were erected and a church was built. Waldo's new agent, Joseph Crell, succeeded in bringing more and more German settlers to New England. He dealt directly with the authorities of Massachusetts, who in 1749 appropriated four townships for the accommodation of foreign Protestants. Two townships were situated in an area which is now Franklin County and also extends into Vermont. The names of the present towns of Adamsville, Bernardstown, and Leyden date back to the German settlements Adamsdorf, Bernardsdorf, and Leydensdorf. The other two townships were to be located in Cumberland County. Since Crell did not succeed in settling one hundred and twenty Protestants in each of the townships within three years, however, the land grants were revoked. Some of the Germans destined originally for those townships settled instead in and around Boston.

In imitation and emulation of Germantown near Philadelphia, New Germantown was founded about ten miles south of Boston (in the present neighborhood of Braintree, Quincy). Two waves of immigration, one in 1750-1751 and another in 1757, swelled the population of New Germantown, which for a time seemed to rival Waldoboro. Even Benjamin Franklin invested in New Germantown by buying a few town lots, thereby expressing his hope for its success. But after seven years of brave attempts to make New Germantown thrive (especially by the establishment of glassworks), the colony broke up and most German settlers moved out to join fellow countrymen in other settlements. Similar migrations were taking place in all the colonies, and German settlers could be found in each of the colonial states before the War of Independence.

3
The Near West

It would have been strange not to find Germans among the early hunters and pioneer settlers going west. People coming from the Valley of Virginia and the mountains of the Carolinas, with their strong German populations, reached the "West" of those days through the Shenandoah Valley. But before the region was permanently settled, we find Germans among its explorers. George Yeager (from the German, Jaeger), who as a child had been captured by the Indians, remembered buffalo hunts in Kentucky and other expeditions he had made with the Indians. He described the richness of the country and the abundance of game in such glowing colors to his two companions, Simon Kenton and George Strader, that the three decided in 1771 to rediscover the paradise of Yeager's youth. They travelled down the Ohio River to the mouth of the Kentucky River without finding the rich cane-lands described by Yeager. Strader was killed when Indians attacked, and the other two fled from Kan-tuck-kee, the Indian name for "the dark and bloody ground." In 1775 after Yeager had also been killed by Indians, Kenton accidentally discovered the region corresponding to Yeager's description—south of the Ohio River within the Blue Grass country.

As early as 1767, two hunters from Pittsburgh, Stoner (also Steiner) and Harrod found abundant game in the bend of the Cumberland, the present site of Nashville. The earliest colonial settlement of Kentucky was Harrodsburg, founded in 1774 by Harrod and some forty men he had led there. The group built cabins and planted corn. According to L. Collins in *Historical Sketches of Kentucky* (1847), the corn was planted and harvested by John Harman (Johannes Hermann) in 1774.

In 1774 Daniel Boone and Michael Stoner were sent by Governor Dunmore to the "Falls of the Ohio," at the site now called Louisville, to lead a party of surveyors safely home. Boone and Stoner had been schoolmates and had grown up together in Bucks County, Pennsylvania. Daniel Boone spoke Pennsylvania Dutch fluently and was said by some to be German since his real name, Bohne, is common in Germany. When Daniel was eighteen he went to North Carolina to farm and hunt. In 1769, together with other frontiersmen, he explored the area between the Ohio, Tennessee and Cumberland rivers. Two years later he returned there with his own and five other families, but hostile Indians drove them back as far as the Clinch River. In 1775, Richard Henderson, head of a company buying and selling land, hired Boone to mark a trail and guide a group of settlers into Kentucky. On that trip Daniel Boone built the fort on the Kentucky River which he called Boonesborough, after his name. He subsequently moved with his family to many spots in Kentucky where, by the 1780s, he was known and respected as Colonel Boone.

Casper Mansker or Mansko was another German trapper and hunter connected with the winning of the Near West. He belonged to the famous "Long Hunters." This group of backwoodsmen left North Carolina in 1769 to hunt further west. Some of them were so fascinated by the wilderness and its abundant game that they did not return for a year—which gave cause for their nickname. Casper went back and forth several times over the Cumberland Mountains to guard and escort parties of settlers or hunters. On those marches no one was allowed to go ahead of him lest they take away the scent. In his broken English he used to say, "I can see pote sides and pehind, too." He was an excellent marksman and Indian fighter. He called his rifle "Nancy." His fondness for "Nancy" was only surpassed by the love for his "gute alte Frau," his good old wife. Once he was almost trapped by an Indian hunter imitating the call of the wild turkey. But luckily for Casper, "Nancy wanted to speak to the Indian," and did so with fatal effect. In his old age, Mansker became an ardent and earnest Methodist.

The tragic experience of two other Germans, Crist and Crepps, and their companions was not uncommon on the frontier. In 1788 they went down the Ohio River on a flatboat on an expedition to prepare salt. The company of twelve armed men and one woman was attacked by Indians in the Salt River. The Indians took the woman captive and killed all the men except for Crist, who, in spite of his wounds, made his way to the salt camp. Though he could not walk, he bound his moccasins to his knees and crawled through briars and thorns to safety. The woman was returned in an exchange of prisoners after General Anthony Wayne's victories over the Indians, and she reported that the party of attacking Indians had consisted of one hundred and twenty warriors. About thirty Indians had been killed. Crist lived to the age of eighty, after having served in the Kentucky legislature and in the United States Congress.

There were other Germans, too many to mention, among the daring hunters and pioneers of other nations. Theodore Roosevelt in *The Winning of the West* gave just tribute to them:

The West was neither discovered, won, nor settled by any single man. No keen-eyed statesman planned the movement, nor was it carried out by any great military leader; it was the work of a whole people; of whom each man was impelled mainly by sheer love of adventure; it was the outcome of the ceaseless strivings of all the dauntless, restless backwoods folk to win homes for their descendants and to each penetrate deeper than his neighbors into the remote forest hunting grounds where the perilous pleasures of the chase and of war could be best enjoyed. We owe

the conquest of the West to all the backwoodsmen, not
to any solitary individual among them; where all alike
were strong and daring, there was no chance for any single
man to rise to unquestioned preeminence.[1]

As we have seen, some Germans were trappers and
hunters exploring the West. The majority of Germans, however, belonged to the class of permanent settlers and farmers.
They chose their land and settled down, instead of restlessly
seeking new frontiers to conquer. They took a lasting interest
in the region they settled, cutting new and better roads
through the forests and farming the land—introducing soil
conservation, crop rotation and fertilization.

In their zeal to build permanent homes for themselves
and their children the Germans did not lose interest in
religion and education. The first institution of higher learning
west of the Alleghenies, Transylvania University, founded
1798 in Lexington, Kentucky, had three German-Americans
among its first trustees: John Bowman (Baumann), George
Muter, and Jacob Froman. To establish a German Reformed
church near Lexington, Germans held the first lottery in
Kentucky.

Through the reports of the Lutheran missionaries of the
North Carolina Synod, we learn that German settlements
spread westward all over Ohio, Kentucky, and Tennessee.
In 1803, when the Reverend R. J. Miller went southwest-
wardly from Abingdon, Virginia, he found several German
congregations established in Sullivan County, Tennessee,
in charge of the Reverend Mr. Smith. Reverend Smith's
predecessor, Reverend Sink (Zink), had left for Kentucky,
undoubtedly to attend to German congregations who had
settled there. Reverend Miller found a number of the congregations on the Holston River. The name of this river is
frequently spelled "Holstein" which suggests the influence
of German population of that region.

Following the Louisiana Purchase of 1803, many second
and third generation Germans from the seaboard states
moved southwest into the Louisiana Territory to secure
homes "without money and without price." The influx of

German settlers was so great that in 1812 the North Carolina Synod admitted nine congregations in Tennessee. By 1820 the Lutherans had become so numerous in eastern and southern Tennessee that they formed a separate synod, the Tennessee Synod.

After General Anthony Wayne's victory over the Indians in 1795, the Ohio Valley also received more immigrants. The Pennsylvania German Ebenezer Zane (Zahn) founded Zanesville on the upper Muskingum. As payment for his lands, he cut a pack-horse trail from the Ohio River at Wheeling to Maysville, Kentucky, by way of Chillicothe. In 1797 the United States mail was carried over this path for the first time. The road remained for a long time the connecting link between the East and Kentucky. In New Lancaster, a town laid out by Zane in 1797, the first German newspaper west of the Alleghenies, *Der Lancaster Adler,* appeared in 1806. When Jefferson County on the right bank of the Ohio was organized in 1797, many Germans settled there and founded the city of Steubenville. The large number of German place names throughout Ohio, such as Berlin, Winesburg, Saxon, Hanover, Strasburg, Dresden, Osnaburg, Frankfort, Spires, Potsdam, Freeburg, and others, indicate a widespread German population. Towns with scriptural names, such as Bethlehem, Salem, and Nazareth, were usually settled by German sectarians, the Moravians, Dunkers, Amish, and others.

Early German settlers in Cincinnati were few but very influential. One of them was Martin Baum, who had come west with General Wayne and later settled down as a merchant in Cincinnati. Baum became very wealthy and supported various kinds of enterprises. He built the first iron foundry in the West in 1810. With the help of Gulich, a German expert from Baltimore, he built the first sugar refinery in Cincinnati, and he founded the city's first bank. Together with another German, Captain Bechtle, he began the use of sailboats on the Ohio and the Mississippi. Martin Baum became mayor of Cincinnati in 1807 and was reelected in 1812. With other public-spirited men he founded the Western Museum in 1817 and Cincinnati College in 1818. He over-

came the financial setbacks of 1821-1822 and established a
cotton trade with Liverpool in 1829. When he died in 1831,
Baum had earned the distinction of having been his generation's greatest pioneer of commerce in the Near West.

Dayton and Germantown were early rival cities in Ohio.
But Dayton outranked Germantown in 1828 when a canal
was built from Dayton to Cincinnati. Two German manufacturers, Gross and Dietrich, who arrived in America in 1828,
later built the Dayton and Michigan Railroad with their own
resources. The line ran from Dayton to Toledo. They paid
nearly three million dollars for this railroad, which covered
a distance of one hundred and forty-three miles. The canal
and railroad boosted Dayton's population to a boom. Outranked Germantown nevertheless remained a strong German
settlement, and though it never achieved large size, it retained its German character. In 1845, all of its five churches
used the German language for religious service.

Most early settlers of Ohio could not enjoy regular
church services, but were visited by itinerant preachers from
time to time. One of those preachers was Heinrich Boehm,
the real apostle of German Methodism in the United States.
Born in 1755 in Lancaster County, Pennsylvania, to Martin
Boehm, bishop of the United Brethren, Heinrich was educated by Rosman, a Hessian soldier who had been captured
with Rall's regiment at Trenton. This education gave Heinrich Boehm above all an excellent command of the German
language. This proved to be of importance and convenience
when, in 1808, he accompanied Bishop Asbury on a missionary tour. "Brother Boehm has the largest body of
hearers, because he preaches in German,"[2] the bishop noted
in his journal.

Boehm preached, in German, at Pittsburgh, Pennsyl-
vania; Wheeling, West Virginia; Chillicothe, Circleville,
Lancaster and Zanesville, Ohio; Frankfort, Lexington, and
Louisville, Kentucky; in several places in Tennessee and
North Carolina, and at Charleston, South Carolina. On Sep-
tember 4, 1808, Boehm preached the first German sermon in
Cincinnati. He remarked in his journal, "The village prom-
ises to grow very rapidly. It has almost two thousand in-

habitants."[3] He later apologized for having called Cincinnati, the "Queen City of the West," a village.

Heinrich Boehm lived to become one hundred and one years old. His centenary on June 8, 1875, was celebrated in Trinity Church, Jersey City, and he preached a sermon for the occasion. He had travelled over one hundred thousand miles on foot and horseback during his missionary tours, witnessing the change from open prairie and forest to fertile farm lands and prosperous towns and cities. From 1796 to 1872 he had voted in all presidential elections and seen all the presidents of the United States from Washington to Grant.

4
The Middle West

The settling of the Near West—Kentucky, Tennessee and Ohio—had been accomplished by first and second generation European-Americans, with German-Americans contributing a good share. The Revolutionary War in America and the subsequent Napoleonic wars in Europe had more or less halted the flow of immigration from Europe to America. With the defeat of Napoleon and the reestablishment of the old absolutist regime on the European continent by Metternich and the Congress of Vienna, the hopes of many Europeans for escape from pressing economic and political conditions were again turned toward the United States. The great wave of German immigration from 1820 until well into the twentieth century reached its crest in 1854 when every second immigrant was a German.

Following the Louisiana Purchase of 1803, New Orleans became an important distribution center for immigrants. Some Germans had settled in New Orleans shortly after its founding by the French in 1718, enticed by a speculator, John Law, to settle in the "earthly paradise of Louisiana" for three years' service as payment for free passage, land, and citizenship. Most of them were camped on the coast of Biloxi near

Mobile Bay, where they remained for about five years, and where hundreds fell victim to southern fever. In 1722 three hundred were settled west of the Mississippi in Attakpas, southern Louisiana, where they became prosperous.

A more fortunate group of Alsatians and Wuertembergers were settled by a Swedish captain, Karl Friedrich D'Arensbourg, in the St. Charles district twenty miles above New Orleans. Place names like Lac des Allemands and Bayou Allemand testify to their existence. The settlements remained important for that region until 1750.

New German immigration during the nineteenth century did not arrive in New Orleans until 1830. While most of the new arrivals were transported to the upper Mississippi, many stayed in New Orleans. The city housed about ten thousand Germans shortly after 1840. Most were not wealthy enough to leave the city during the fever season, and almost a thousand died in one year, 1843. The Germans who lived in Algiers, opposite New Orleans, were prosperous and could, therefore, enjoy a more carefree life under the southern sun. In general, however, the climate of the lower Mississippi did not favor German immigration, although there were German settlements in St. Peters, Baton Rouge, and on the Red River as well as in the towns of Alexandria, Natchitoches, and Shreveport.

Next to New Orleans, St. Louis was the second most important center of distribution of settlers for the Western territory. Settlements spread quickly to the north and south on the Missouri and Illinois sides of the Mississippi River, and upstream along the Missouri which stretched out into the West like a long pointing index finger. Many Americans of German blood from the Eastern states settled there. One of them, Henry Geyer from Frederick, Maryland, was a noted lawyer and later became a United States senator from Missouri.

The first two Germans from abroad to visit Missouri were Gottfried Duden, a graduate in law and medicine, and Eversmann, an agriculturist. In 1824 they landed at Baltimore, and left from there for St. Louis in search of suitable farmland. Both settled down in what is now Warren County above the Femm-Osage River, about fifty miles above the mouth of the Missouri. Duden could afford to have his land cleared and cultivated. For three years he led the comfortable life of a gentleman-farmer. In 1827, he returned to Germany where his reports about his trip and his experiences were widely read and induced many people to emigrate. How could those who lived in meager circumstances in Germany resist trying the good life in America after hearing Duden's description?

> As long as the settler does not have sufficient meat from the domestic animals, the hunting grounds keep him in provisions. Flesh of the domestic animals is, to be sure not dear here; a pound of ox flesh costs only one and one half cents, and pork, two cents. But there are so many deer, stag, turkeys, hens, pigeons, pheasants, snipes and other game that a good hunter without much exertion provides for the needs of a large family. Throughout the whole United States, hunting and fishing are entirely free, and in the unenclosed spaces anyone can hunt when and how he pleases, small as well as large game, with dogs, slings, nets and rifles. There are two varieties of deer here in Missouri, and they are for the most part very fat. The meat is savory, but the hunter rarely takes the whole animal with him. He is satisfied with the hind quarters and the skin, and hangs the rest of the animal on a tree so that someone else can take home a roast if he pleases. Wild turkeys are found in droves of twenty to fifty. They are especially fat toward Christmas. I have my neighbor deliver some to me every week for soups, for I am not a good hunter.[1]

The Missouri made famous and attractive by Duden's pen soon became known not only for German farmers and laborers but also for people of a higher social class—counts and barons, scholars, preachers, students, merchants, and officers. Those accustomed to hard work prospered after years of toil and labor, while the others failed utterly, some of them committing suicide, some dying as beggars on the street. But all cursed Duden as a *Luegenhund*, a lying dog.

In 1834 a group of university men under their leaders Paul Follen and Friedrich Muench came to the United States to fulfill their dream of establishing a true democratic German state here. Their attempts to bring about political liberty and union in their own country had been thwarted by tyrannical decrees. Moreover, they were watched by an Argus-eyed system of espionage. These conditions led to the formation of the Giessen Emigration Society, which was named after the German university city in which it was founded. They were true patriots, leaving Germany only to realize their dream, expressed by Paul Follen in this way:

> We must not go from here without realizing a national idea or at least making the beginnings toward its realization; the foundation of a new and free Germany in the great North American Republic shall be laid by us; we must therefore gather as many as possible of the best of our people about us when we emigrate, and we must at the time make the necessary arrangements providing for a large body of immigrants to follow us annually, and thus we may be able, at least in one of the American territories, to establish an essentially German state, in which a refuge may be found for all those to whom, as to ourselves, conditions at home have become unbearable, . . . a territory which we shall be able to make a model state in the great republic.[2]

Faced with the realities of pioneer life, they never obtained the fulfillment of their dream. How could they? E. D. Kargan, a member of the Giessen Society, described the group as follows:

> They had wielded the pen, but never had handled the hoe; they had stood in the pulpit but never behind a plow; they had lectured from the cathedra* and pleaded in court, but had never driven an ox-team. They were but little prepared for the hardships that were in store for them.[3]

The group arrived at New Orleans not knowing where to turn for the realization of their goal. They went to St.

---

*Probably corrupted from the original German *Katheder,* meaning, in this context, "the lectern of a professor."

Louis where some of the members remained. Muench and
Follen settled near Marthasville, in Warren County, near
the site of the farm which had been owned by Duden ten
years before. Muench recalled:

> We found already living here a party of Westphalian la-
> bourers, who had made the necessary preparations, and a
> mixed aristocracy of German counts, scholars, preachers,
> economists, officers, traders, students and others, and many
> more arrived during the following years.[4]

Those people had become accustomed to the life in the
country and were fully occupied to make a living for themselves and their children. Thoughts of establishing a German
state in Missouri were far from their minds because they had
severed the ties with "the old country." By 1848, even Muench
agreed with his neighbors and quietly abandoned his earlier
ideals:

> We almost repented of having given up our Fatherland as
> hopeless, and would willingly have thrown ourselves into
> the struggles there, but already we and our families had
> taken deep root in the new world.[5]

Muench's idealism did not falter completely. Practical
as he was, he shifted his ground from the idea of a New
Germany to the attainable aim of giving German flavor to
American life and strengthening the influence of the German
people in American affairs. The settlement of the Giessen
Society in Warren County, Missouri, became the nucleus of
German settlements on both sides of the Missouri River,
starting from its mouth to one hundred and twenty miles
westward, from St. Louis to Jefferson City.

Another attempt to establish a "New Germany" in Missouri was made by the Philadelphia German Settlement Society in 1836. The motivation behind this venture seems to
have been more economic than patriotic; it was a way to earn
money from land sales. The society bought eleven thousand
acres from the government for $14,000, and three hundred
acres from private owners for $1,535 in Gosconade County.

They selected a town site on the south bank of the Missouri
River about seven miles east of its confluence with the Gas-
conade River. The project was extensively advertised in the
United States and in Germany. The town proposed to serve
as the center of the settlement was named Hermann in honor
of a German hero, who in 9 A.D. had defeated three Roman
legions under their leader Varus. The high expectations
tendered for Hermann by the Philadelphia Settlement Society were never fulfilled, but the modern visitor may still
find "A Bit of the Old, in the Heart of the New." Such was
my impression when my family and I visited Hermann in
the summer of 1973, and I agree with the statement made by
Samuel F. Harrison in a historical sketch about the city:

> Though not completely German nor larger than Phila-
> delphia as the German Settlement Society had hoped,
> Hermann has kept much of her Old World charm. With her
> modern shoe factory and other industries, the future looks
> promising. Worthwhile projects promoted by civic organi-
> zations with the cooperation of the city administrators in-
> clude a swimming pool, construction of an area hospital,
> $80,000 improvements of the City Park, increased tourism
> as well as other phases of community betterment and beau-
> tification. The churches, most of which have their roots
> going back over a century, provide an inspirational at-
> mosphere for the town. The teachers in the schools, many
> native, provide a rewarding education thought so essential
> by the town's founders. So this then is Hermann, Little
> Germany, the Wine City of Missouri, The City Beautiful,
> Home of the "Maifest."[6]

The Germans populating the Missouri Valley in great
numbers differed in religion, being Catholics, Protestants,
and Sectarians. The vastness of their new home-country
made all draw together, however, and they became tolerant
of each other. A delightful story illustrating the unity of the
multi-faith German towns is told about a prominent German
settler, J. B. Bruhl. Bruhl was a Catholic living in a Protestant township. Since the settlement lacked any ordained
ministers, Bruhl served all of the colonists, regardless of

their denomination, as a sort of minister-teacher. As soon as the Lutherans became more numerous, they asked the patriarchal Bruhl to get them a Lutheran minister; and he did. The Catholic Bruhl even heard out the trial sermons of candidates for the Lutheran pulpit in his district and generously expressed his recommendations.

The German farmers in Missouri took good care of their farms and their animals, keeping the land in the family's possession generation after generation. In many instances the Germans had bought the farms from their slave-owner Anglo-American neighbors. After visiting Hermann in 1855, Franz Loeher remarked, "Their Anglo-American neighbors are being bought out, thanks to the Germans, who give them dollars for their improved land, and then they proceed deeper into the backwoods to clear new ground."[7] Loeher notes with satisfaction that the Germans in Missouri did not themselves own slaves and that wherever Germans settled, slavery tended to disappear: "in the neighborhood of Hermann too, the land of the slave-owners is being gradually bought up."[8] There is no question that the gradual disappearance of slavery in Missouri (because of the influx of antislavery German farmers) helped, among other factors, to keep Missouri within the Union during the Civil War.

Some members of the Giessen Society who did not settle with Muench and Follen in Missouri or remain in St. Louis crossed the Mississippi to the east to settle in Illinois, which had been admitted into the Union in 1816 and was not a slave state. They favored St. Clair County and settled in or near Belleville, about fifteen miles southeast of St. Louis. They found there a German settlement already flourishing. Before 1820 Belleville claimed two German families, the Maurers and the Bormans. (The latter had come from Pennsylvania and had changed their name from Bornmann when they moved to Illinois.) During the twenties only a few German families settled in the county, but in and after 1829, Germans arrived in great numbers, attracted by the land's rich mixture of woodland and prairie. From about 1832 onward German settlers filled an entire township (thirty square miles), five to ten miles east of Belleville. In 1832 at Turkey Hill the brothers Hilgard founded the nucleus of the famous "Latin Farmer" colony which attracted many educated immigrants from Germany. Members of the *Burschenschaften,* the German student fraternities who were driven out of their homeland because of their liberal political views, settled there. Men like Dr. G. Engelmann, Dr. G. Bunsen, Dr. A. Berchelmann, Gustav Koerner and others made and kept the area for a long time a "Little Germany." Belleville was almost completely a German city during the nineteenth century. The mayor and most members of the city council were German; three of its five newspapers were printed in German, and many of the local blacks spoke German.

Friedrich Hecker, leader of the revolutionary forces in Baden, Germany, came to the United States and bought a farm near Belleville in 1849 after the revolution in Germany had been crushed. He became a good neighbor of Gustav Koerner with whom he had fought a duel during his university days in Germany. Gustav Koerner was lieutenant-governor of Illinois in 1852 and minister to Spain from 1862 to 1865. He did not belong to the Giessen Society and did not advocate the formation of a German state in the New World. Rather, he warned his fellow German immigrants saying:

> He who leaves Europe permanently must bid farewell to all museums, galleries, Gothic monuments, gardens and theaters, which have perhaps given him so much many-sided enjoyment, and must console himself ... with the green of thick forests and the flowering of the wide prairies.[9]

Other southern Illinois counties which received early German settlers were Madison and Bond Counties. Vandalia, which in 1819 was the capital of the state, was founded by a group of Germans from Hanover under their leader, Ernst. In the early 1830s Alton, Madison County, was the most important commercial city in Illinois because of its proximity to St. Louis. Many Germans settled and prospered there. With the end of the Black Hawk War in 1832 and the building of railroads, the central and northern areas were opened for settlement. Quincy, Springfield, Peru, Beardstown, Peoria, and Galena way up in the northwest corner of the state received good shares of German settlers. The first mayor of Galena, Stahl, was the son of German parents residing in Baltimore. Franz Arenz, an important businessman, settled in Beardstown. Georg Wolf settled in Quincy in the summer of 1822, one year after its first settler, John Wood, arrived there. Wolf bought the land from Wood, who later became the governor of the state. Many so-called Saxon Lutherans— most of them farmers from Pomerania—settled in the 1840s in the southern counties of Washington, Randolph, and Monroe.

Meanwhile, Chicago gradually grew more and more important. When it became a city in 1837 and elected its first officials, there were eighteen Germans among the voters. A baker, Matthias Meyer, is said to have been the first permanent German inhabitant of Chicago. By 1848 Chicago had scarcely ten thousand inhabitants. In the same year the German weekly the *Illinois Staats-zeitung* was started, while in contrast, St. Louis had already two German dailies. The Germans of Chicago remained politically alert during the nineteenth century. In 1844 a first meeting was held in Chicago in opposition to the nativistic influences. The Chicago Germans reached the height of their political influence in the days of Franz A. Hoffmann, merchant and banker, who was an ardent supporter of Abraham Lincoln and who became lieutenant governor of Illinois in 1860.

Indiana received German and German-Swiss settlers as early as 1790. The Swiss settlement of Vevay was founded in 1796. French-Swiss winegrowers supported by German farmers tried to grow vine on the Ohio River. In 1810 they had their first good vintage year, producing about twenty-four hundred gallons of wine, followed by a production of five thousand gallons in the peak year of 1817. Their hopes to surpass and to supplant the French wines, however, were never realized. On the contrary, the colony gradually declined, and many of its best men left Vevay for Cincinnati. Captain Weber was one of them. He founded the Wilhelm

Tell Hotel in Cincinnati, which for some time enjoyed an excellent reputation.

The most interesting German settlement in Indiana was New Harmony on the Wabash River in Posey County, settled by a society founded by sectarian Johann George Rapp, a native of Wuerttemberg. The Harmonists, or Rappists as the members of this society were called, believed that the world was coming to an end before the nineteenth century was over. In 1803, "Father" Rapp and his followers left Germany to seek refuge in America. They founded the colony of Harmony in Butler County, Pennsylvania, where they lived and prospered until 1815. Selling their property for $100,000, they bought new land on the Wabash River and founded New Harmony. Father Rapp not only was the spiritual leader of the community, but also kept a tight hold on the purse strings. By contract every member, man and woman, turned all profits over to Father Rapp, who provided for them in sickness and old age. According to his biographer Marguerite Young, "Father Rapp chose America first—not because he believed God's voice would speak out of the marsh more clearly than it had spoken out of the vineyards of Wuerttemberg—but because the land was fierce and cheap. Father Rapp had a Bible in one hand and an ax in the other. . . ."[10]

Father Rapp did listen to God's voice in Indiana, where he believed God spoke to him through the voice of an angel. A footprint preserved in a slab of stone in the barley fields along the Wabash was Rapp's proof of the angel's appearance, and the message he delivered was that God would send flames from heaven and poisonous gases from the center of the earth to destroy everything and everyone except New Harmony—which would become the New Jerusalem with ten gates of jewel-studded gold. Father Rapp even furnished a description of the angel to his awestricken followers. The angel was taller than an oak and had a rainbow on his back. He held seven stars in his right hand and seven golden candlesticks in his left. He wore a linen robe adorned with rubies, sapphires, and emeralds and spoke in a voice that roared like a storm.

The men and women of the Harmony Society lived a celibate life "as brothers and sisters in Christ." The New Harmony colony in Indiana continued to thrive under the leadership of Frederick Rapp, an adopted son of Father George Rapp. Frederick combined artistic qualities with the shrewdness of a businessman. He painted pictures, composed hymns, and collected Indian relics when he wasn't directing the usual business of the society, the sale of whiskey, hides, fur, livestock, shingles, butter, flax, hops, tobacco, hemp, furniture and fruits of all kinds. In 1820 the property of New Harmony was valued at over a million dollars. John Woods, who lived twenty miles away from the colony of New Harmony in 1820, made the following observations about its inhabitants:

> They were amazingly similar. The men wore jackets and pantaloons, very wide, of vivid Prussian blue, with coarse flat hats like pancakes. The women wore jackets and petticoats, a darker shade, with skullcaps and straw bonnets. . . . The Rappite people, marching in unison, two by two, waved their sickles in distant greeting as they passed, as if they had been given a signal to do so.[11]

After ten years in Indiana, the Harmonists decided to move back to Pennsylvania. Historians suggest several reasons for this move: the prevalence of malaria in Indiana, difficulties with meddlesome neighbors, the fact that Robert Owen, father of English socialism, was ready to buy out the community, and above all, the members of the Harmony Society wanted to expand and get closer to the Eastern market after they had decided to concentrate on manufacturing rather than agriculture. Under the leadership of Frederick Rapp, they founded Economy, Pennsylvania, in 1825. It was situated on the Ohio about eighteen miles from Pittsburgh. Again the settlement prospered. In 1831, they manufactured woolen goods valued in excess of $84,000 and that of cotton was nearly $17,000. Frederick Rapp died in 1834; George Rapp, the founder of the society, died in 1847 at the age of ninety. Since the society enforced celibacy, its membership decreased steadily, until in 1903 only four members, one man and three women, were left. A syndicate of Pittsburgh capitalists bought the property for $2.5 million.

In Iowa, settlement was rapid from 1842 onward. The good soil and fine climate of Iowa attracted not only native German-Americans but also new German immigrants from abroad. In the first three months of 1842, 529 steamers had come to St. Louis bringing more than thirty thousand passengers to Iowa. Since the Mississippi River served as the entrance road to Iowa, the cities of Keokuk, Burlington, Davenport, and Dubuque sprang up on its banks. The discovery of lead in the vicinity of Dubuque attracted many settlers. Peter Weighle, a German who came to Dubuque in 1832, was the first white man to settle there after the French fur traders had left. Catholics as well as Lutherans came to Iowa and formed large congregations by 1880. The Germans of Iowa were interested in politics and furnished five of the ten state councilmen. Several Germans became county supervisors. J. H. Thedings, born in East Frisia, Prussia, exemplified the political ambitions of the Iowa Germans. He was, in turn, justice of the peace, mayor, president of the county council, and head of the school system.

Michigan in its northern and western parts remained for some time untouched by European settlement because of a cold climate and the presence of hostile Indians. The German element, however, was represented in those regions by a Catholic missionary, Friedrich Baraga. Born in Austria in 1797, he decided in 1830 to work among the American Indians. In Cincinnati, he learned the language of the Ottawa Indians from a native attending a Catholic school of that city. Establishing himself at Arbre Crochu in the northern part of Michigan, he taught the Indians of Lake Superior "the three R's" and also the basic principles of Christianity. Baraga became bishop of the Northern Indian Missions in 1853, residing in Sault Sainte-Marie. He wrote his own textbooks and catechisms in the Chippewa language and compiled a grammar of the Chippewa dialect and a reader in the Ottawa language. Friedrich Baraga concluded his life in the service of the Indian missions at Marquette, Michigan, in 1869.

Dr. A. Hammer, another Catholic priest and missionary, wrote in 1829 concerning the German settlements in Michigan:

> Real German life as it is found in many American states, one can find in Michigan only in three places, for in all other places our people [meaning the Germans] are too scattered to form congregations that might support a German Preacher: (1) In Detroit there are two large German congregations, the stronger being Catholic and having built a cathedral, the other, also having a church of its own, being Protestant (the Reverend Mr. Schade). The members of the two congregations live in harmony with each other, and never allow their religious differences to interfere with their social intercourse. At marriages and baptisms they are never concerned about which preacher they should choose, but that they should have a good time in the German fashion. A large number of the Germans remain in the city only so long as to earn money enough to buy land outside and establish farms. (2) The second German colony, and the most prosperous, is that near Ann Arbor. The Germans there come largely from Wuerttemberg, and are under the Protestant preacher, the Reverend Mr. Schmid. Their grain and cattle are unsurpassed in Michigan. (3) The third German colony is that on the Grand River, in the neighborhood of Lyons, Ionia County, under the Reverend Mr. Kopp, from Westphalia. The colony is called Westphalia.[12]

From the travelogues by J. G. Kohl we learn a few more facts about the Ann Arbor Germans:

> The first were some few who came from the villages near Stuttgart about 1830. It was just the time when Michigan was lauded to the skies, just as twelve years later everybody talked about Illinois and Indiana, and after another twelve years, it was Iowa, Wisconsin, and Minnesota. The early settlers helped build the city of Ann Arbor, and wrote home about their prosperity. The word was passed from village to village; first a dozen men, then a dozen families, crossed the ocean until about five to six thousand Swabians had settled around Ann Arbor (1855). The native

speculators had bought up the land near the prosperous settlers, but the increased price of land did not stop the purchasers, for the Swabians kept on extending their farms. Detroit's German newspaper, already in existence toward the end of the forties, did not prosper greatly until the large German immigration of the fifties was added to the Michigan population.[13]

5
The Northwest

The successful campaign against the Indians in the Black Hawk War of 1832 opened the Northwest Territory for increased settlement. The soldiers who took part in these military expeditions spread the good news about the mineral wealth and fertile soil of Wisconsin. The state grew rapidly from 3,635 inhabitants in 1830 to 2,069,042 inhabitants at the census of 1900. At that time, the population of Wisconsin was 34.3 percent German.

The Funk family of seven were the first known Germans settling in Green County, Wisconsin, where the "Funk" blockhouse was established among the pioneer stations in 1832. Beginning in 1840, Germans arrived in great numbers in Wisconsin, with Milwaukee serving as a distribution center. During the summer season of 1843, more than a thousand German immigrants arrived each week.

Prominent among the immigrants to Milwaukee was F. W. Horn, who had become a member of the first legislature by the time Wisconsin became a state in 1848. Horn also subsequently became speaker of the House in 1851 and continued to serve in the legislature until as late as 1882. Other noted Germans included three men among those delegated

to form Wisconsin's constitution in 1846: Dr. Franz Hueb-
schmann and two Germans from Washington County, Jann-
sen and Kern. A printer, Moritz Schoeffler, founded the
first German weekly in Wisconsin in 1844, *The Wisconsin
Banner,* which later became a daily paper.

German-American churches and schools grew up rapidly. When the Catholic church established a bishopric in
Milwaukee in 1844, many Catholics of the southern states of
Germany were drawn to Wisconsin. Dr. Joseph Salzmann, an
Austrian priest, founded a Catholic seminary, St. Francis,
outside Milwaukee. Soon a teachers' seminary was added,
which trained many German teachers for various parts of
the country. The Lutheran churches and schools were also
numerous and active. Two of the early prominent Protestant
colleges founded by German-Americans were Northwestern
University at Watertown and Concordia Gymnasium at Milwaukee. In 1851 the Deutsch-Englische Akademie was
founded in Milwaukee, and it became well known throughout the country for the work of its director Peter Engelman,
who instilled his love for teaching in many generations of
students.

By the mid-1800s Milwaukee had acquired a distinctly
German flavor. Turnvereine, singing societies, and theatrical
groups were formed, and the German beer brewers, Schlitz,
Pabst, Blatz, and Miller, saw to it that everyone had a good
time. Besides breweries, Germans entered into other industrial enterprises. Their tanneries, tobacco storehouses, banks,
and hotels and their trade in iron, lumber, and pharmaceutical products not only built the wealth of Milwaukee but also
gave the state of Wisconsin a leading position in the commerce of the Great Lakes and the Northwest Territory.

R. G. Thwaites, secretary and superintendent of the
State Historical Society, details the distribution of Germans
in Wisconsin in his annual report of 1890:

> The Germans number seventy-five percent of the popula-
> tion of Taylor County, sixty-five percent of Dodge, and
> fifty-five percent of Buffalo. They are also found in espe-
> cially large groups in Milwaukee, Ozaukee, Washington,

Sheboygan, Manitowoc, Jefferson, Outagamie, Fond du Lac, Sauk, Waupaca, Dane, Marathon, Grant, Waushara, Green Lake, Langlade, and Clark Counties. There are Germans in every county of the state and numerous isolated German settlements, but in the counties named these people are particularly numerous. Sometimes the groups are of special interest, because the people came for the most part from a particular district in the fatherland. For instance, Lomira, in Dodge County, was settled almost entirely by Prussians from Brandenburg, who belonged to the Evangelical Association. The neighboring towns of Hermann and Theresa, also in Dodge County, were settled principally by natives of Pomerania. In Calumet County there are Oldenburg, Luxemburg, and New Holstein settlements. St. Killian, in Washington County, is settled by people from Northern Bohemia, just over the German border. The town of Belgium, Ozaukee County, is populated almost exclusively by Luxemburgers, while Oldenburgers occupy the German settlement of Cedarburg. Three fourths of the population of Farmington, Washington County, are from Saxony. In the same county Jackson is chiefly settled by Pomeranians, while one half of the population of Kewaskum are from the same German province. In Dane County there are several interesting groups of German Catholics. Roxbury is nine tenths German, the people coming mostly from Rhenish Prussia and Bavaria. Germans predominate the Cross Plains, the rest of the population being Irish. The German families of Middleton come from Koeln, Rhenish Prussia, and so did those of Berry, a town almost solidly German.

In 1952 when I first arrived in America, Milwaukee still possessed much of its German flavor. Viewing Milwaukee from my train window was in itself comforting to me and much like a home-coming. On the long train ride from New York, typical American cities like Buffalo, Detroit, and Chicago had a strange look to a German newcomer like me. The landscape and towns presented a pleasant and more familiar appearance as we rode through Kenosha and Racine to Milwaukee, where I felt almost at home. I had arrived shortly before Easter, and the German singing societies were holding their spring concerts and dances. My knowledge of English was rather limited since I had forgotten much of my four years of German high-school English studies. German relatives and friends in Milwaukee made the transition period easy for me.

When I entered the University of Wisconsin, Milwaukee, to study English, Latin, and German, and to prepare for a high-school teaching career, my instructors showed much understanding for my situation. I remember that I wrote a note to my professor of general psychology asking that I not be called upon in class "because I can't express myself in English very well." Because she responded with understanding and did not embarrass me, I felt all the more obliged to study hard and pass all my written tests. I found Milwaukee and its German community well accustomed to newcomers from Germany, and the long tradition of their welcome to these newcomers made it relatively easy for me to start anew in a strange country.

In the nineteenth century, Minnesota developed almost as rapidly as Wisconsin. It had only 6,077 inhabitants in 1850 which number tripled by 1858, when Minnesota was admitted as a state. The German element became the largest foreign element of the state, followed by Norwegians and Swedes. Historically, the most interesting German settlement of Minnesota is New Ulm on the Cottonwood River, a tributary of the Minnesota River. New Ulm was founded in 1854 and was at that time the westernmost settlement of the Minnesota Territory.

The first settlers were members of the German Land Association founded in Chicago by Frederick Beinhorn. The purpose of the German Land Association was to resettle scores of German immigrants who flooded the labor market in Chicago. Exploitation of immigrant labor prompted the Settlement Society of the socialistic Turner League to search for land to re-settle their unemployed or underemployed members. In 1857 the Turner League bought the land of the New Ulm, Minnesota, settlement from the German Land Association of Chicago, and the two projects merged. This merger swelled the population, and New Ulm was incorporated as a town of Minnesota Territory in the same year.

Wilhelm Pfaender and Jacob Nix were the leaders of the new community. During the Sioux uprising of 1862, Jacob

Nix was commandant of the defenses of New Ulm, which was to take the heat of the attack since it was the western-most town. The Indians attacked at a time when most able-bodied men had enlisted in the Union army. Families in the outlying farms were slaughtered outright or tortured to death, and only the reinforcements from Fort Ridgely saved New Ulm from suffering greater losses than their eight killed and seventy wounded.

Wilhelm Pfaender was a member of the Minnesota State Legislature in 1859. At the outbreak of the Civil War he joined the Union Army and distinguished himself as com-mander of a battery of artillery. When he learned about the Sioux attack on New Ulm he hurried to St. Paul where he found his family as refugees, but unharmed. In Minnesota he joined a newly formed Minnesota cavalry regiment. He later became a lieutenant colonel at Fort Ridgely in charge of the border defense. From 1865 to 1869 he worked his farm, exchanging the sword for the plowshare. Pfaender be-came a state senator in 1869, and when he returned after his term to New Ulm he was elected mayor of the town. He also served a four-year period as state treasurer, from 1875 to 1879, before he settled down to a quiet life with his family in New Ulm.

The settlement of New Ulm had started as an experi-ment in community ownership, but began to prosper only when it changed to a free enterprise system. The Turner Society members were in general free-thinkers, caring little about orthodox religion. They remained, however, very tol-erant when a Catholic and a Protestant parish were estab-lished in New Ulm. From the memoirs of the Catholic priest, Father Berghold, we learn that the local brewer, in spite of his religious indifference, offered one of his buildings for religious service when the church was partially destroyed by a storm, and that other free-thinkers did not mind occasion-ally having a glass of beer in the clubhouse with Father Berghold. The six-member school board of New Ulm, ac-cording to an unwritten law, always consisted of two free-thinkers, two Catholics, and two Protestants.

6
The Southwest: Texas

Other attempts at forming a predominantly German region were made in Texas, shortly after Texas had won independence from Mexico in 1836. A society by the name of "Germania," founded in 1839 in New York, had aimed to establish a German colony in Texas. Galveston was to become the distribution center for the immigrations to follow. However, the first attempt at settlement failed because of the murderous climate of the fever-infested harbor city. The society dissolved in Houston, leaving the poorer members there to shift for themselves, while the president and the well-to-do members returned to New York.

In 1842 several German noblemen formed a company for the settlement of Germans in Texas on a large scale. Texas had won independence from Mexico in 1836 and remained a free government until 1845 when it became part of the United States. The *Mainzer Adelsverein,* as the company was called, made the following proposition to the Texan government through Colonel Daingerfield, representative of the Republic of Texas at The Hague and in certain German free cities:

1 The Society would engage itself
(a) To introduce to Texas and to settle there within a
certain period of time from 1,200 upward to ten thousand (10,000) German families and single men or about
that number suiting the wishes of the Government.
(b) To negotiate at suitable terms and with the necessary guarantee a loan of one million dollars to the profit
of said Government.
(c) To obtain for the respective governments of Germany the permission for the subjects of the Republic of
Texas to import the new products of the country under
moderate tolls and customs with the estates belonging
to the German Customs—(Zoll-Verein).
2 Whereas the Government of Texas on its side would
engage itself
(a) To yield to the Society a grant in proportion to the
number of immigrants fixed in the contract to be
granted, colonized on the same terms and conditions
here-to-fore made with especial regard that all lands
fit for cultivation shall be omitted.
(b) To allow the Society as such, besides the free introduction or importation of the property of the single
settlers, to import free from any charge or custom during a longer period of time to be fixed in the contract,
productions of Germany to the amount of $200,000 per
annum. Mentz [sic] September the 14th., 1843. Au-
thorized by the Society for Protecting German Settlers
in Texas. (Signed Charles, Prince of Solms, Victor
Count of Leinigen, Charles Count of Castell.)[1]

In 1844, Prince Charles of Solms-Braunfels, one of the
signers of the above proposition, left Germany for Texas,
followed by one hundred and fifty families. After their arrival at year's end in Lavaca Bay, they were transported in
ox-carts through trackless and swampy areas to the banks of
the Comal River. There, in March of 1845, they founded New
Braunfels, named in honor of their leader. Since the company of *Adelsverein* was granted three hundred and twenty
acres for every male settler and six hundred and forty acres
for every family, it could have become extremely profitable
under good management. But Solms-Braunsfel proved to be

an incompetent manager. He squandered much of the company's resources and returned to Europe leaving the funds of the *Adelsverein* almost exhausted. Braunsfel's successor, Baron von Meusebach, wisely economized by enforcing cutbacks in the company's support of the settlers. He nevertheless succeeded in founding another settlement, the city of Fredericksburg, situated about ninety English miles from New Braunfels. But when the *Adelsverein* sent thousands of new settlers from Germany, without a penny for their upkeep or transportation, from Galveston to New Braunfels, even the energetic Baron von Meusebach could not cope with the situation. The twenty-five hundred immigrants had to shift for themselves. Many of them succumbed to the fevers and excesses of the tropical climate. Others sought work in Galveston, where barons were reduced to pushing wheelbarrows or doing other menial jobs. Moreover, Texas was now part of the United States, and the country was on the verge of a military invasion against Mexico. All available means of transportation were requisitioned by the military forces, denying the Germans all hope of getting to New Braunfels. Several hundred of the new immigrants, therefore, joined the United States army that invaded Mexico.

The few who made it to New Braunfels were faced with a strange situation. Many of the inhabitants grew indolent and shiftless in spite of good harvests, because they were used to receiving supplies from the *Adelsverein*. Others, unaccustomed to the climate, became ill and tried to drown their miseries in pleasure. Every night they joined the well-off in a dance hall where clarinet music was provided by the colony's professional gravedigger. Many deaths occurred; corpses were said to have piled up at the door of Dr. Koester, the company's doctor and only physician of the settlement. People referred jokingly to the cemetery as "Koester's plantation." New arrivals from Germany during the summer of 1846 raised morale, and New Braunfels eventually triumphed over the odds against it, and developed into a prosperous community.

With Texas becoming a state of the Union, any political aspirations of the *Adelsverein* to make Texas, or at least part

of it, a "Little Germany" came to an end. With the help of
Queen Victoria and Prince Albert of England, to whom some
of the leaders of the *Adelsverein* were related (Victor Count
of Leinigen was Queen Victoria's half-brother, and Charles
of Solms-Braunfels her uncle), the company of the *Adelsverein* had tried to keep Texas out of the Union and make
it a predominantly German independent and feudalistic state.
The company sold its properties and finally dissolved in 1853.
The colonists then had to make it on their own and most of
them prospered. Though the company venture had failed,
if it had not been for the *Adelsverein,* probably not as many
Germans would have settled in Texas. By 1850 the population of Texas was about twenty percent German. San Antonio, Dallas, Galveston, Houston, and Austin received a
good portion of German immigrants, and many German
farmers settled within the triangle between Seguin, New
Braunfels, and San Antonio.

7
The Far West

The expedition of Lewis and Clark in 1804-1805 had opened the way to the Far West. But at first no settlers followed their path—only some trappers and hunters. In the early 1820s members of Congress claimed that the country's natural boundary was the Pacific Ocean. The swelling tide of our population was to roll on until that mighty ocean interposed its barrier, and limited the territorial empire. The government was powerless to prevent the spread of population to the Pacific Coast. Western expansion was our "manifest destiny." Thus, in 1840, the United States government initiated a program of planned settlement of vast regions stretching west from the Mississippi to the Pacific Ocean.

John C. Fremont was the foremost pathfinder for the settlers moving west. He covered twenty thousand miles on his excursion trips into the unknown western wilderness. The importance of those trips lies above all in the fact that Fremont brought back maps and topographical sketches of the regions he had investigated. A German surveyor, Charles Preuss, who had studied geodesy in Germany and had been a surveyor for the Prussian government, was hired by Fremont as topographer. Preuss accompanied Fremont on ex-

peditions in 1842 and again in 1843. Fremont was the first one
to acknowledge Preuss's accomplishments saying, "To his
[Preuss's] extraordinary ability and skill I owe the continuous topographical sketches of the regions through which
we came. . . ."[1]

The U. S. Senate commissioned Preuss in 1847 to make
a map of Oregon and Upper California, which, when finished,
became one of the topographical milestones of American
history.

The settling of the Oregon Territory started about 1839.
A decade later, however, Oregon lost many of the original
settlers to California because of the gold rush. To stem the
flood of settlers leaving Oregon for the south, Congress decreed that every male inhabitant who had settled in Oregon
before the first of December, 1850, should receive three hundred and twenty acres of land and a similar amount for his
wife; settlers from December 1, 1850, to December 1, 1853,
should receive one hundred and sixty acres, plus an equal
amount in case they were married. The condition attached by
Congress was that the settler must remain for four years.
These inducements by Congress kept many settlers in Oregon. They preferred the life of the well-to-do landowner to
the harassed and uncertain life of the gold seeker. Portland,
the commercial center of Oregon, had many German inhabitants whose descendants keep German traditions and culture
alive to this day. From their arrival, the Germans in Portland founded singing and gymnastic societies, contributing
to the social and cultural life of the city.

In 1853 the Oregon Territory was divided. The territory
north of the Columbia River was called Washington. Seattle,
the most important city of the Washington Territory, was
founded by a Maryland German, Henry L. Yesler. Born in
Leitersburg, Maryland, in 1811, he later learned the trade
of carpenter. At the age of twenty he settled at Massillon,
Ohio, and became rich by his industry and thrift. When the
boom hit the Pacific coast he went there by ship, sailing from
Baltimore to Panama, and, after crossing the isthmus, taking
a ship to California. He did not linger in California or Oregon, but went straight to Washington, the "only real lumber

country in the world," as he was told. Arriving in the fall of 1852, he took advantage of the government grant in obtaining one hundred sixty acres for himself and the same amount for his wife. In the summer of 1853 he built a sawmill on the present site of Seattle to establish trade with San Francisco. Yesler, by exploiting low-cost Indian labor, became very rich. He was, nevertheless, liked by his Indian employees and became their popular patron. Thus, he succeeded in keeping the Indians of Washington Territory at peace during the Indian troubles of the 1860s. He later became mayor of Seattle and remained for many years its leading citizen.

Besides furnishing their quota of gold-seekers, quite a few Germans also contributed to California's wine industry. Pioneers in that field were Gundlach, Dresel, and Krug. Gundlach and Dresel established the "Rhine Farm" in 1858 near San Francisco. Charles Krug settled first near Sonoma, becoming the first wine grower of Sonoma Valley. When he married the niece of General Vallejo, his bride brought him a five-hundred-forty-acre vineyard as part of her dowry. Krug's wines were considered the best in California during the second half of the nineteenth century. When he died, however, his famous winery passed to other hands. Employees of Charles Krug began their own wine businesses and made good on their own, as, for example, Carl Wente and the Beringer brothers.

Germans also made a name for themselves in the cultivation of fruit trees in California. Anaheim, twenty-eight miles from Los Angeles, was founded and settled by Germans. Many southern fruits were cultivated there, including the oranges for which Anaheim became famous. The Francher Creek Nurseries in Fresno County were founded by Frederick Roeding; his son, George C. Roeding, continued the family business and contributed to the cultivation of the fig and other fruit trees. George Roeding wrote a book entitled *California Horticulture* and authored a monograph on fig cultivation. For a time a German by the name of Rose owned one of the finest plantations of fruit trees near Mission San Gabriel.

Los Angeles, San Francisco, San Bernardino, San Diego, Santa Barbara, and Anaheim contain large German populations. A number of German industrialists contributed to the economic wealth of California. Karl M. Weber founded the Stockton Mining Company in Stockton, San Joachin County. James Lick, born in Pennsylvania of German parents, is best known as the founder of the Lick Observatory in San Francisco. Contributing to the wealth of San Francisco were Germans Claus Spreckels, the "sugar-king," Henry Miller, the "cattle-king," and his partner, Charles Lux.[2]

The plains and plateaus of the arid West were settled after the Civil War when railroads became the prevailing means of transportation. Most Germans who settled in the prairie region between the Mississippi and the Rockies were of Russian-German stock. In spite of their century-long stay in Russia, these immigrants were essentially German and had kept their German language and customs. Catherine the Great of Russia, originally a German princess, had invited those Germans, who came mainly from West Prussia, and had granted them special privileges in Russia, most importantly freedom from military service. When the Russian government subsequently cancelled their exemption from military service, they felt compelled to leave Russia for America. The Mennonites were especially concerned because they refused military service on religious grounds.

A little more than ten percent of those Russian-Germans leaving Russia were Mennonites. The others, mostly Lutherans and some Catholics, were attracted by offers of employment by American railroad companies as well as by promising opportunities in agriculture and the sugar industry. The first group of Russian-Germans from the Black Sea area arrived in the United States in 1847-1848 to grow grapes at Kelly's Island, Ohio, and to farm in Iowa. Several groups settled in Nebraska in 1873, and Lincoln, Nebraska, became the center of the Volga Germans. The Russian Mennonites kept closely together and formed large settlements in Kansas between 1876 and 1878. In Kansas, as well as in the Dakotas, the Russian-German farmers generally became very successful. They adapted quickly to the new way of life and learned how to use American machinery on their farms, which varied in size from sixty to a thousand acres.

The bread basket of America and the world is still being filled to a large extent by the diligent and productive work of the farmers of the Middle and Far West. The German-Americans who settled there formed a major part of one of the greatest farming cultures the world has ever known.

German immigrants, as well as second and third generation native-born German-Americans, followed the frontier west until they reached the ocean, carrying their values of diligence, productivity, and frugality with them and influencing the development of American culture from coast to coast.

8
German-Americans in Business and Sports

The opening of the vast territories west of the Mississippi brought great opportunities to enterprising pioneers. Following the route of Lewis and Clark along the Missouri to the Columbia River to the Pacific Ocean were trappers, or "mountain men," as they were popularly called. They mainly trapped beaver and sent the pelts to St. Louis, the busy fur market in the Midwest.

Outstanding among those who prospered by the fur trade was John Jacob Astor, son of a poor farmer. Astor was born in Germany in 1763 at Walldorf near Heidelberg. He first worked on his father's farm where he learned the trade of a butcher. At the age of sixteen he joined his brother George in London. There the two brothers produced and sold musical instruments. In 1783 John arrived in New York where he worked as a butcher with his older brother Henry. When John Jacob married Sarah Todd, cousin of the eminent Brevoort family, she brought a dowry of $300 with her, which Astor invested in the fur business, convinced that the outside of an animal would bring him more profit than its meat. Tenaciously following the rules he had set up for himself— to be industrious and not to drink or gamble—the German butcher became a wealthy and powerful man in the fur business. In 1809, with a capital of $500,000 he organized the American Fur Company, which became the first monopoly on the North American continent. In 1811, Astor sent the sailboat *Tonquin* south from New York around Cape Horn, and then up the coast to the mouth of the Columbia River in the Oregon Territory. There the thirty-three trappers on board founded a trading post for fur, which they named Astoria.

Astor's bold jump to the Far West enabled the United States to lay claim to the Oregon Territory, which at one time was claimed by four nations—Spain, Russia, Great Britain, and the United States. During the War of 1812 the British took Astoria and named it St. George. After the war, however, it was returned to the United States. Spain, in 1819, and Russia, a few years later, relinquished their claims to the Oregon Territory. England and the United States then jointly held claim until 1846. In that year Britain and the United States agreed on the 49th parallel boundary from the Rockies to the Pacific Ocean.

Despite setbacks during the War of 1812, Astor had continued to expand the fur trade. From St. Louis he sent an expedition of sixty-seven experienced trappers westward to establish tradeposts along the way to Astoria. Indians were the main suppliers of furs, and they usually got the losing end of the deal. On one occasion Astor traders exchanged two dollars' worth of useless trinkets for a load of furs which were sold for $20,000 to Chinese mandarins. Soon Astor realized that the fur trade had reached its climax, and he was clever enough to invest in the real estate business. For a time, nearly half of Manhattan was his, and he became the "Land-Lord of New York." Although John Jacob Astor was the richest man in North America by 1835, he continued to live plainly and soberly above his office, salesroom, and fur warehouse at 223 Broadway, in New York City. At his death in 1843, his fortune was estimated at $20 million. He founded the Astor Library in New York with a gift of $400,-000, and his son, William Backhouse Astor, further enriched its holdings by adding to it Alexander von Humboldt's pri-

vate library in 1865. The well-known writer Washington
Irving was a personal friend of John Jacob Astor. In his
novel *Astoria* Irving preserved the story of his friend's ven-
tures for posterity.

Another German knight of fortune was John August
Sutter, who arrived in California in 1839. The governor of
Mexico, Juan Baptista Alvarado, granted Sutter the right
of citizenship and title to fifty thousand acres of land. Sutter
became governor of the Northern Frontier Territory of
Mexico, and received permission to build a fort at the Sacramento River, the site of which was later to become the capital of the State of California. Born in the Grand-Duchy of
Baden in 1803, Sutter had been trained in the military
academy of Bern, Switzerland, and served for a time in the
French army. In 1834 he had arrived at New York, and for
some years had carried on a caravan trade between St. Louis
and Santa Fe. In 1838 he travelled with a party of trappers
to Vancouver, and after various adventurous trips to Alaska
and the Sandwich Islands and cruises along the Pacific coast,
he had been driven by a storm into the Bay of San Francisco.

With the help of Indian friends and the government of
Mexico Sutter founded the settlement on the Sacramento
River. He taught the Indians European agriculture, established artisan shops, and became somewhat of a feudal baron
of the self-sustaining settlement. In his employ were also
two Germans, Henry Huber, who was in charge of agriculture, and Charles Flugge, who was Sutter's lawyer.

Sutter at that time had become the richest man in the
California Territory; but the rural idyll of his colony and his
riches were to come to a sudden end. It was just a few days
before the Treaty of Guadalupe Hidalgo was to be signed
between the United States and Mexico, making California
a part of the United States. James Marshall, one of Sutter's
employees, found gold on the south fork of the American
River while building a sawmill. It was January 20, 1848. Sutter tried in vain to hide the find, but his land was soon invaded by gold-seekers of every nation who devastated his
fields and slaughtered his cattle. The titles to his land were
disputed and Sutter became a poor man, until the State of

California voted him an annual pension of $3,000 during the years 1865 to 1872, for the taxes he had paid on the lands he no longer possessed. Sutter, the pioneer who had laid the foundation for the fortunes of thousands of people, remained relatively poor.

Among the fifty thousand "Argonauts" who streamed into California to find gold were two brothers. Charles and Hugo Nahl were descended from a family of artists. Their great-grandfather, Johann Nahl, had been an important artist of the German rococo period; and their father, George Valentin Nahl, was a well-known engraver. Both brothers studied under Vernet in Paris until the revolutionary movements in the 1840s brought them to America. They stayed only a short time in New York before following the gold-seekers to California. They sketched and painted the turbulent life on and off the gold fields. In addition they designed not only the famous bear flag of California but also its great seal. Today, Charles Nahl is considered to have been the leading artist of the Gold Rush.

The German Claus Spreckels made his fortune in the sugar business. Born in 1803 in Hannover, Germany, he made himself the "sugar king of the West" by importing sugar cane from the Hawaiian Islands. Before he established the California Sugar Refinery in 1863, he had returned to Germany to work in a sugar refinery at Magdeburg. He returned to California with new ideas in the sugar business, introducing the sugar cube and granulated sugar to the American market. The Hawaiian Islands furnished his business with a steady and inexpensive supply of raw material. Spreckels managed also to become the good friend of Kalakua, the unpredictable king of the Islands. According to one story that circulated in San Francisco and was widely believed, Spreckels had won the island of Oahu in a poker game with Kalakua. That was, of course, a very tall story. Nevertheless, Claus did return to the mainland with a lease on twenty thousand acres of land which he later increased to one hundred thousand acres on which he raised sugar cane.

The Eastern Sugar Trust was Spreckels' greatest competitor. The Eastern Trust attempted to ruin Spreckels by selling sugar in the West at a loss. However, Spreckels had enough money to buy a large refinery in Philadelphia and undercut the price of sugar in the eastern markets. The Eastern Sugar Trust finally backed out, buying Spreckels's Philadelphia refinery and promising to stay out of the western markets. By 1888 Spreckels was the unchallenged sugar king of the Pacific Coast. He immediately spread out into other enterprises, including the California Railroad, electric power and gas companies, and the Oceanic Steamship Company. When Claus Spreckels died in 1908 his fortune was estimated at $15 million in addition to the Spreckels' building, the first skyscraper of San Francisco.

The Havemeyers of New York had established themselves as the reigning sugar family of the East long before Spreckels was established in the West. The ancestors of the family, William and Frederick Havemeyer, emigrated from Bueckeburg, Germany, and established themselves as sugar-refiners in New York City. William Havemeyer arrived here in 1799; his brother Frederick in 1802. Their sons continued the family business which had a capital of $75 million in 1909. William F. Havemeyer, a grandson of the first Havemeyer, was thrice elected mayor of New York.

The throne of "lumber king" was claimed by Frederick Weyerhaeuser who came to the United States in 1852 as a penniless youth. He did not care for the title, which was bestowed upon him by the newspapers. To the contrary, he went about the business of amassing tens of millions of dollars quietly, and with extreme reticence about publicity. Weyerhaeuser started as a worker in Illinois sawmills, but soon realized that he could not become rich by sawing lumber for other people. He obtained his fabulous wealth partly by his German trait of economy and partly by appreciating, not merely exploiting, the rich timber land, which he harvested by adhering to a strict program of preservation. The rest he perhaps owed to his friendship with James J. Hill, operator of the Northern Pacific Railroad. Their mansions were built next to each other in St. Paul, Minnesota.

The Weyerhaeuser Lumber Company bought valuable

forest land from the Northern Pacific at bargain rates, contributing much to the wealth of the company. When Frederick Weyerhaeuser died in 1914, his fortune was estimated at $300 million; but following the principle of discretion set by the founder, the Weyerhaeuser family tried to conceal the glare of all that money from the public eye. Their attempts were in vain; and in 1935, George, the nine-year-old great-grandson of Frederick Weyerhaeuser, was kidnaped. The boy was ransomed for $200,000, an amount the spokesmen for the family asserted could be raised only with great difficulty.

The Northern Pacific Railroad was the source of wealth for another enterprising German, Henry Villard (Heinrich Hilgard). Born in 1835 in Speyer, Germany, he completed the western extension of the Northern Pacific, thus creating a trunk-line stretching from the Great Lakes to the Pacific Ocean. As the representative of the foreign bondholders of the Oregon and California Railroad Company he was chosen the company's president in 1875; but acquiring wealth as one of the great railway magnates was not Villard's only interest. In 1858 he reported the debates between Lincoln and Douglas, and established himself in Washington as political correspondent for the leading eastern papers. For three years during the Civil War he served as a war correspondent, and later became the publisher of the New York *Evening Post*. Among other prominent German-Americans Henry Villard was a member of the Reform Club of New York City, founded in 1888. The Reform Club tried to contain the abuses of capitalism lest the system be smashed by the rise of political and social revolt. In apparent reference to the Reform Club and to similar clubs like The Sound Money League of Pennsylvania, Andrew D. White, United States Ambassador to the German Empire, said in a speech on May 22, 1897:

> History will record it as a pregnant fact that the vast mass of Germans have been on the right side of the financial questions which in recent years have so agitated this country. Whether they have called themselves Republicans or Democrats, they have been almost to a man opposed to all wild fiscal experiments, to all financial tricks and efforts to

outwit the eternal laws of nature, to the "greenback craze," to the "silver craze," and to all those outbursts of unreason which for a time have seemed to threaten the future of this country.[1]

Henry Villard's philanthropic activities led the way for many other millionaires of the robber-baron period, when they decided to atone for their sins of public exploitation by acts which would improve their public image. Villard gave generously to a number of universities, including the State University of Oregon, the University of Washington State, and Harvard University. In addition he endowed several philanthropic institutions in Germany: a hospital and training school at his birthplace Speyer, an orphan asylum at Zweibruecken, a new hospital of the Red Cross in Munich, and an industrial institution at Kaiserslautern.

One millionaire moved by the example of Henry Villard was John D. Rockefeller, founder of the Standard Oil Company. His $32 million gift to the General Education Board was "the largest sum ever given by a man in the history of the race for any social or philanthropic purposes" up to that time. In 1906 John D. Rockefeller erected a monument to the memory of his ancestor Johann Peter Rockefeller, "who came from Germany about 1733 and died in 1783." The monument stands in the village of Larrison's Corner, near Flemington, Hunterdon County, New Jersey. Supposedly, the Rockefeller family descended from a Huguenot ancestor, who had immigrated to Germany. To this day members of the Rockefeller family are active in politics and philanthropic activities.

Another German industrial giant was the inventor George Westinghouse, who made travel by train safer at the time when railroads were extended from the East Coast to the west. His sure-fire air brake saved thousands of lives. Westinghouse was born in 1847 in upper New York State. His German parents were farmers and not very well off. While still in his teens, he fought bravely on the battlefields of the Civil War. An inventor at the age of twenty-two, with a shrewd business instinct to combine with his talent, George

Westinghouse became a powerful magnate by the time he was thirty. But, as his friend Nikola Tesla testifies, he did not let success go to his head:

> Like a lion in the forest he breathed deep and with delight the smoky air of his factories. Always smiling and polite, he stood in marked contrast to the rough and ready men I met. And yet no fiercer adversary than Westinghouse could have been found when he was aroused. An athlete in ordinary life, he was transformed into a giant when confronted with difficulties which seemed insurmountable. He enjoyed the struggle and never lost confidence ... had he been transferred to another planet with everything against him he would have worked out his salvation.[2]

Another German inventor who "worked out his salvation" against obstacles was Charles Steinmetz. Born in Breslau, Germany, in 1865, he had a hunchback that made him appear like an over-sized dwarf, but his brilliant mind and his ability in the field of electrical engineering more than made up for his physical handicap. His love for drinking beer and for comradeship made him join a socialist student fraternity, the only fraternity to accept him. Although Steinmetz was not a socialist fanatic, he was subsequently hunted by the German secret police and forced to leave his homeland. The immigration officials in New York refused his entry. If it had not been for a Danish-American student whom Steinmetz had met on the voyage and who now vouched for him, Charles Steinmetz, who would one day be known as the wizard of Schenectady, would have been returned to Germany. Instead, Charles entered New York and went to work for a fellow countryman, Rudolf Eickemeyer, who was running a small Yonkers factory which produced hat-making machines. Eickemeyer was trying to develop a workable electric motor, and Steinmetz was just the right man for the job. In fact, he developed more than two hundred inventions which reduced the magnetic losses in electrical motors and generators and protected high-power transmission lines from lightning. By 1902, Steinmetz was a recognized authority in the electrical field. Harvard recognized him with an honorary degree as the "foremost electrical engineer in the world." He agreed to work for General Electric on the condition that the company buy out his former employer, Eickemeyer. His reputation at General Electric as a genius was well established, and he was referred to as "The Supreme Court."

When the new generator at Ford's River Rouge plant did not work properly, Steinmetz was called to fix it. He walked around the generator humming to himself. He then simply made a chalk mark on one side of the generator and asked the workers to remove the plates there and take exactly sixteen windings from the coil. He charged Ford $10,000 for his trouble, and when the surprised Ford asked for an itemized statement, Steinmetz obliged: "Making chalk mark on generator, $1. Knowing where to make chalk mark, $9,999."

Charles Steinmetz contributed in large measure to the comfort of modern society through his inventions. His human qualities, however, were even more appealing. He filled his laboratory with pets likely to be physical outcasts as he had been: a Gila monster, snakes, seven alligators, and two crows which sat on his shoulders. One cold winter day he sat bundled up in his lab refusing to light a fire, because a mouse with its litter had occupied the furnace, using it as a nursery. Since Steinmetz had early resolved never to marry, he adopted the entire family of his assistant, Joseph Hayden. The Haydens had three children, and Steinmetz loved his role as foster-grandfather.

There was nothing more important to "Grandpa" Steinmetz than reading bedtime stories to the children. Once he made Henry Ford, who wanted to discuss an urgent problem, wait until he had finished the story he was reading to his "grandchildren." Steinmetz's death in 1923 was a great loss for General Electric; his adopted family felt the loss even more.

Many German names can be found in the American world of sports. The attraction to science which made many German-Americans become famous inventors may also have attracted others to the sport of baseball because of its geometric order, its requirement of technical skills and discipline. In his excellent book, *The German-Americans,* Richard O'Connor proposes an all-star German-American team which would, he believes, be hard to beat: Lou Gehrig, first base; Frank Frisch, second base; Honus Wagner, shortstop; Heinie Groh, third base; Heinie Manush, left field; Bob Meusel, center field; Babe Ruth, right field; Ray Schalk, catcher; and Rube Waddell, pitcher.[3]

Rube Waddell was an outstanding pitcher whenever he decided to play, and not go fishing or on a beer drinking spree instead. The management of the club as well as the fans were never sure whether Rube would show up for a game. Sam Crawford, Waddell's teammate on the Detroit Tigers, recalls that there was always a commotion in the grandstands and shouts of "Here comes Rube!" when Waddell did appear. Waddell raced through the stands and then "he'd jump down onto the field, cut across the infield to the clubhouse, taking off his shirt as he went. In about three minutes—he never wore any underwear—he'd run back out on the field in uniform all ready to pitch. . . ."

Peter (Honus) Wagner is well remembered by his former teammates. Not too long ago Rube Marquard, pitcher of the New York Giants, remarked:

> Honus could play any position except pitcher and be easily the best in the league at it. He was a wonderful fielder, you know, terrific arm, very quick, all over the place grabbing sure hits . . . you'd never think it to look at him, of course. He looked so awkward, bowlegged, barrel-chested, about two hundred pounds. And yet he could run like a scared rabbit. He had enormous hands and when he scooped up the ball at shortstop, he'd grab half the infield with it. . . . Talk about speed. That bowlegged guy stole over seven hundred bases in the twenty-one years he played in the big leagues. A good team man, too, and the sweetest disposition in the world. The greatest ballplayer who ever lived, in my book.

Wagner's lifetime batting average at .344 was actually higher than that of Babe Ruth.

George Herman Erhardt Ruth, called the "Babe," was
born in Baltimore. He still represents what former sports
writer Paul Gallico called him:

> ... purely an American phenomenon ... an American Por-
> thos ... a Golem-like monster ... the greatest single attrac-
> tion in the entire world of sports ... Ruth's nickname,
> "Babe," is so much part of our national consciousness that
> the strange message spelled out in letters six inches high
> across the top of any afternoon newspaper, "Babe Conks
> No. 36" or "Bam Busts Two," is not, as an English or
> French cryptologist might imagine, a code for "Come home,
> all is forgiven," but a very simple presentation of the news
> that Ruth hit his thirty-sixth home run, and that he has
> made two homers in one game.

It is probably hard for us today to imagine that the
Babe's illness, from eating too many hot dogs and consuming
too many bottles of soda pop, became a national disaster. As
reported by Mr. Gallico, in those days nothing was as big
in the news as Babe Ruth

> hung between life and death for many days—on Page One.
> Bulletins were issued from the sickroom. Little boys
> brought nosegays, or congregated outside the high walls
> of the hospital and looked up at the window of the room
> wherein lay the stricken hero. The presses lay in wait with
> pages of obituaries, and editorials announced the impend-
> ing catastrophe as a national calamity.... He recovered, he
> convalesced, and the nation sent a great sigh of honest
> relief.

Babe Ruth and Lou Gehrig, sons of German immigrants,
were the "home run twins" of the New York Yankees, a
team very successful in the late twenties. As the story goes,
the twins so scared the Pittsburgh Pirates in batting practice
before the 1927 World Series that the Pirates lost the Series
in four straight games.

Both Ruth and Gehrig spoke German well. When sports-
writer Fred Lieb exchanged a few sentences in German one

day with Lou Gehrig, Ruth joined readily in the conversation. The stories about Babe Ruth are plentiful—his rare appetite for beer and steaks, his lust for women. What those stories have in common is that they are told with a smile by friends and foes of the "Babe" alike. Babe Ruth shared the fate of many German-Americans—he was a fellow not altogether liked, but still someone to be admired.

Herman "Germany" Schaefer was another successful and very colorful baseball player. He was known for his refusal to take the "national pasttime" seriously. Once, as a pinchhitter in the 1906 season, he stepped out of the batter's box and addressed the crowd, "Ladies and gentlemen, you are looking at Germany Schaefer, better known as Herman the Great, acknowledged by one and all to be the greatest pinch hitter in the world. I am now going to hit the ball into the left-field bleachers."

In spite of the jeers arising from the crowd, Schaefer did hit a home run into the left-field bleachers on the second pitch. Schaefer, moreover, rendered himself immortal in the history of baseball by being the first and last man to steal first base. The unusual feat occurred in the 1908 season in a game between the Detroit Tigers (Schaefer's team) and the Cleveland Indians. With Schaefer on first and Davy Jones on third, Sam Crawford came to bat in a late inning. Schaefer called for a double steal, but the Cleveland catcher hung onto the ball, and while Schaefer stole second, Jones stayed on third. Davy Jones recalls the sequence of events to follow:

On the next pitch Schaefer yelled "Let's try it again!" And with a blood-curdling shout he took off . . . back to first base, and drove in headfirst in a cloud of dust. He figured the catcher might throw to first—since he evidently wouldn't throw to second—and then I could come home same as before. But nothing happened. Nothing at all. Everybody just stood there and watched Schaefer, with their mouths open, not knowing what the devil was going on. Me, too. Even if the catcher *had* thrown to first, I was too stunned to move. . . . But the catcher didn't throw. In fact, George Stovall, the Cleveland first baseman, was playing way back and didn't even come in to cover the bag. We just watched the madman running the wrong way on the base path and didn't know what to do.

The umpires were just as confused as everybody else. However, it turned out there wasn't any rule against a guy going from second back to first, if that's the way he wanted to play baseball, so they had to let it stand.

So there we were, back where we started, with Schaefer on first and me on second [sic]. And on the next pitch darned if he didn't let out another war whoop and take off *again* for second base. By this time the Cleveland catcher evidently had enough, because he threw to second to get Schaefer, and when he did I took off for home, and *both* of us were safe.

What followed might be called the "Schaefer decision." Ban Johnson, the league's president, decreed a new rule by which the men on base had to run counter-clockwise. The game was saved, and no one could steal first base again.

9

The Forty-Eighters
and the Turner Societies

In the middle of the nineteenth century the wave of German immigration reached its crest—in 1854 every second immigrant was German. Among these new immigrants from Germany was a small but very influential group, the so-called Forty-Eighters. The name refers to those Germans who participated in the various German revolutionary movements in the first half of the nineteenth century. The year 1848 saw the climax of those movements which had tried to replace the absolutistic rule in Germany by a more democratic one. All the movements had failed and refugees of those revolutionary attempts were commonly called Forty-Eighters, though some of them came to the United States as early as the 1830s and early 1840s.

The German Forty-Eighter was distinguished from other immigrants first by outer appearance. Usually male, in his early or late twenties and unmarried, his physical condition was excellent because he had trained his body with gymnastics. He sported student attire or dressed like Friedrich Hecker, the romatic hero of the Revolution, wearing a broad-brimmed hat, a shirt open at the neck, and a loosely tied scarf. His hair was long and wavy, and he had grown a mustache or even a long, full beard. In contrast to his fellow immigrant farmer and craftsman, his hands did not show any sign of physical labor. His luggage was usually slight, consisting in some cases of only one satchel bulging with books and papers. He normally did not go to the rural communities, but rather joined student friends who had preceded him to the cities where they found jobs in keeping with their training as teachers, journalists or even lawyers.

The greatest service the Forty-Eighters performed for their fellow German-Americans was that of filling the void of political leaders in the generally apathetic, apolitical German-American community. The very name "German-American" dates back to the time of the German Forty-Eighters. It did not exist before 1848, and in our time the hyphen has either disappeared completely, or, if it is still used, has lost its sharp edge. In the middle of the nineteenth century, however, the hyphen was used as a sword to defend the German-American against the connotations of nativism.

It was fortunate for the German-American community that the politically interested Forty-Eighters arrived at the height of American nativism. With the attempt to form a third American party—because neither the Whigs nor the Democrats could fight against foreign influence for fear of losing their foreign voters—the nativists became politically active. The so-called American party held its first convention on July 4, 1845, and adopted a "declaration of principles" which read in part:

> The danger of foreign influence, threatening the gradual destruction of our national institutions, failed not to arrest the attention of the Father of this Country, in the very dawn of American Liberty. Not only its direct agency in rendering the American system liable to the poisonous influence of European policy—a policy at war with the fundamental principles of the American Constitution—but also its still more fatal operation in aggravating the virulence of partisan warfare—has awakened deep alarm in the mind of every intelligent patriot, from the days of Washington to the present time.[1]

The main aim of the nativists was to make it more difficult for immigrants to become American citizens with the right to vote, in keeping with the nativists' general attitude that foreign immigrants were inferior to native-born Americans.

In 1854 Congress passed the Kansas-Nebraska Act, opening these territories to slavery. The amendment to this bill by Senator John M. Clayton of Delaware stated quite frankly that slaveholders would be more welcome in the new territories than free immigrants from Europe, and thus joined the two issues of slavery and nativism. Friedrich Kapp, a leading abolitionist in New York, grasped the situation accurately and stated: "The problem of slavery is not the problem of the Negro. It is the eternal conflict between a small privileged class and the great mass of the non-privileged, the eternal struggle between aristocracy and democracy."[2]

Stephen A. Douglas, the author of the Kansas-Nebraska Bill, was branded as "an ambitious and dangerous demagogue" at a meeting of Germans in Chicago on March 16, 1854. Hoffman, a former friend of Douglas, said of him, "He has betrayed the trust which people have placed in his hands." Referring to Clayton's nativistic amendment to the bill, the Chicago meeting of Germans denounced the amendment as "the Devil's cloven hoof sticking out without covering." The meeting further resolved that in the amendment, "We perceive a spirit particularly inimical to us Germans, pioneers of the West as we are; that we have lost our confidence in and must look with distrust upon the leaders of the Democratic party in whom, hitherto, we had confidence enough to think that they paid some regard to our interests."[3] Senator Douglas was hung in effigy for his betrayal of the Germans.

When Senator Adams of Mississippi learned of the indignity offered to Senator Douglas by a German mob, he decided to introduce a bill, increasing the period of probation for immigrants to twenty-one years. Moreover, the Homestead Bill which provided free and cheap land to newcomers was restricted to the heads of families and to citizens of the United States. An ultimate blow to the loyalty of the Ger-

mans to the Democratic party was delivered by Senator Butler of South Carolina during the debate of the Kansas-
Nebraska Bill. He specifically excluded his Irish constituents
and referred in particular to "Germans coming from Bremen," saying, "The intelligent and judicious master, having
his slaves around him in Missouri or Nebraska, would be as
acceptable a neighbour to me and, as I thought would be to
Iowa, as one of those new immigrants."[4] The *Philadelphia
Public Ledger* printed the statement, "Judge Butler declared
frankly in his seat that he should prefer Negroes in Nebraska
to 'emigrants from the land of the Kraut.' "[5] All these incidents alienated the Germans from the Democratic party
and were, according to F. I. Harriot, "a major cause in disturbing their political alignments, shaking and almost shat-
tering their loyalty to the Democratic party, with which
three-fourths of the Germans were then affiliated, inducing
secessions in large numbers in 1856, and it set in motion
among them forces in opposition to slavery, that made the
Germans a determining factor in the overthrow of the Democratic party in 1860 and in the election of Abraham Lincoln."[6]

Senator Butler's outspoken remarks caused the German
voters in Iowa to favor the Whig candidate Grimes for governor in 1854, giving Iowa its first and last Whig governor.
The Whig platform in Iowa avoided the question of slavery,
but had a "dry" plank and was also tainted with nativism,
two issues hated by the Germans. But the Germans voted for
the Whig candidate, because they were more afraid of the
stronger strain of nativism brewing in the powerful Democratic party. The issues in Iowa reflected a national situation.
The new Republican party coming into existence about this
time was in the beginning mainly formed by antislavery
Whigs. As soon as the new party softened its stand on nativism and puritanism, Germans swelled its ranks.

In 1859, however, Republican leaders in Massachusetts
proposed a "Two-Year Amendment" to the state constitution which added two years to the five year probation period
for immigrants. When the voters ratified the amendment,
the Germans in the Republican party became understand-
ably concerned. Republican leaders in other states were

quick to denounce the Massachusetts amendment. Above all, Abraham Lincoln's letter to Dr. Theodor Canisius, editor of the Springfield, Illinois, *Staatsanzeiger* did more than anything else to calm the tension:

> Dear Sir:
>   Your note asking, in behalf of yourself and other German citizens, whether I am for or against the constitutional provision in regard to naturalized citizens, lately adopted by Massachusetts, and whether I am for or against the fusion of the Republicans and other opposition elements, for canvass of 1860, is received.
>   Massachusetts is a sovereign and independent state; and it is no privilege of mine to scold her for what she does. Still, if from what she has done an inference is sought to be drawn as to what I would do, I may without impropriety speak out. I say then, that as I understood the Massachusetts provision, I am against its adoption in Illinois, or in any other place, where I have a right to oppose it. Understanding the spirit of our institutions to aim at the *elevation* of men, I am opposed to whatever tends to [degrade] them. I have some little notoriety for commiserating the oppressed condition of the Negro; and I should be strangely inconsistent if I should favor any project for curtailing the existing rights of *white men,* even though born in different lands and speaking different languages from myself. . . . I have written this hastily, but I believe it answers your questions substantially.
>
> Yours truly,
> A. Lincoln[7]

Lincoln wrote this letter on May 17, 1859. It was reprinted widely by the English and German press. Between 1848 and 1871 more than thirty German periodicals were printed in Chicago alone, and in 1873 almost three hundred daily or weekly publications found readers in twenty-eight states.

On May 30, 1859, Lincoln secretly bought the Illinois *Staatsanzeiger* for four hundred dollars. Canisius remained the editor as long as the paper remained a faithful mouthpiece of the Republican party. Lincoln, seeking the presiden-

tial nomination of the Republican party, was perhaps showing concern about the German vote by buying the Canisius
printing establishment. Historians have hotly debated
whether or not Lincoln owed his nomination and the presidency to the German vote. It is true that many Germans,
especially in the rural districts, had remained Democrats,
and that Lutheran as well as Catholic German-Americans
were against the anticlerical Forty-Eighters who were for
Lincoln and the Republican party. It is equally a fact that
neither Lincoln nor Douglas received many, if any, votes
from Germans who had settled in the Southern states.
Nevertheless, it is safe to conclude that the political influence of the Forty-Eighters on their fellow Germans helped
Lincoln to win both the nomination of his party and the
presidency.

Lincoln may have been even more closely linked to the
German-Americans by his own ancestry. A. B. Faust states
in *The German Element in the United States,* "A theory has
been advanced to the effect that the ancestry of Abraham
Lincoln was German, based upon the fact that his grandfather's name appears on a Land Office treasury warrant
(No. 3334) as Abraham Linkhorn. The discovery has occa-
sioned a controversy which is by no means clearly settled."[8]
In a footnote attached to the name Abraham Linkhorn in the
quote above, Faust substantiates this claim as follows:

> The argument was first made by Mr. L. P. Henninghausen,
> a most diligent and successful investigator of the historical
> records of the Germans in Maryland (author of the *History
> of the German Society of Maryland*). A facsimile of the
> land warrant, contained in the land office at Richmond, is
> printed in Nicolay and Hay, *Abraham Lincoln,* vol. 1, p. 10
> (see also p. 14) and reprinted in the *Eleventh and Twelfth
> Reports of the Society for the History of Germans in Mary-
> land,* pp. 37-42. The name Abraham Linkhorn is very
> clearly and distinctly written, and reappears, moreover, in
> Record Book B, p. 60, in the office of Jefferson County,
> Kentucky, on a surveyors certificate, May 7, 1785. Abra-
> ham Linkhorn was a man of some means and education,
> was killed by the Indians, and his son Thomas, father of

the sixteenth president of the United States, grew up without schooling or paternal care amid coarse frontier sur-
roundings. The name Linkhorn could not, as has been
conjectured, be a clerical error for Lincoln. The very genealogical investigation by J. H. Lea and J. R. Hutchinson
The Ancestry of Abraham Lincoln, (Houghton-Mifflin
Company, 1909), takes no account of the "Linkhorn document," which omission destroys its value in the controversy. It attempts to give a very complete genealogical
chain, leading through Massachusetts ancestry back to a
family of Lincolns in England. Abraham Lincoln did not
know of any connection with the Massachusetts family, but
said that his ancestors had come from Berks County, Pennsylvania, and Rockingham County, Virginia, and thence
to Kentucky, and that his people were non-combatants.
The latter would mean that they were sectarians,—Mennonites or Quakers. Both Berks County, Pennsylvania and
Rockingham County, Virginia, were German counties, and
the census of 1790 gives several instances of the name
Linkhorn in the German counties of Pennsylvania. On tax
lists of the county of Northumberland, 1778-80, and 1786,
appear the names Hannaniah Linkhorn and Michael Linkhorn, respectively; Jacob Linkhorn is named on the tax
lists of the county of Philadelphia in 1769. Cf. *Pennsylvania Archives,* vols. XIV and XIX.[9]

Whether of German ancestry or not, Lincoln was a great
American president and an even greater human being. As
president, he showed himself very grateful to the Forty-
Eighters who had supported him. Canisius was appointed
consul to Vienna in 1861 and later served in the same post at
Bristol, England, and the Samoan Islands. Georg Schneider
served as consul in Elsinore and successfully spread the
cause of the Northern states during the Civil War in the
Scandinavian countries. Koerner succeeded Carl Schurz as
minister to Spain, when the latter returned to the United
States to fight in the Union army. Koerner executed his
assignments well by preventing European recognition of the
Confederacy and by furthering friendly relations with Spain.
Friedrich Hassaurek was appointed minister to Ecuador and
resided at the capital city of Quito, which lies between nine

and ten thousand feet above sea-level. Hassaurek thanked
the president for appointing him to "the highest position the
administration had power to give." Lincoln liked the pun
and shared it with his cabinet and friends.

There were numerous other Forty-Eighters and German-
Americans loyal to the Republican party who were awarded
consular and state offices after 1860. A noteworthy exception
is the Chicago physician Dr. Ernst Schmidt. He was popularly called *der rote Schmidt* on account of his red hair and
socialist leanings. He ran for mayor of Chicago on a Socialist
ticket in 1859 and received twelve thousand votes out of
twenty-eight thousand. When Friedrich Hecker called on
Lincoln at the time of the Inauguration, the president is said
to have asked, "What became of that long, red-haired Dutchman, Dr. Schmidt? Almost every Dutchman has been here
asking for a job; why doesn't he come in?"

One of the finest tributes to the Forty-Eighters was
made in a speech by Dr. Edmund J. James, former president
of the University of Illinois, at memorial services for Carl
Schurz in Chicago, June 3, 1906:

> We were approaching the crisis in our national history
> when we were to determine whether this nation was still
> to continue half slave and half free, or whether it was to
> continue at all or not. Speaking as one whose ancestry
> unto the fifth and sixth generations have been born and
> died on American soil, speaking as one whose genealogical
> roots run deep into the Southland and far into the North,
> I believe that if the struggle had been left to what might
> be called the purely American elements as they existed
> in the '50s in the United States, the outcome might have
> been different from what it was. We who love to com-
> promise, that characteristic of the Anglo-Saxon, might
> have tried to worry on under some kind of system by which
> slavery should have increased in power and strength with-
> out weakening the vigor and might of the free states—
> of course, an absolutely hopeless proposition. Or we might
> have consented to a possible dissolution of the Union,
> which would have been a great misfortune, entailing upon
> our children and children's children untold and undreamed
> of miseries. But the men of '48 who had come into leader-

ship of this great and ever increasing throng of German-
Americans were men not bound down by any of those traditions which held us in chains. They knew nothing of the
Missouri compromise or the Nebraska bill or any other of
the numerous devices by which we tried to break the
force of the coming storm. They were men who had suffered on behalf of liberty; they were men who had staked
their entire careers on the side of freedom in the great
struggle between privilege and democracy; they were
prophets; they were seers; they were idealists; they saw
or thought they saw what was right, and they planted
themselves firmly and distinctly on that side with no hesi-
tation and no wavering. They rallied to a man to the standard of the Union and of freedom.

The influence of the Forty-Eighters at this great and
critical time of our national life was, to my mind, decisive.
They turned the balance of power in favor of union and
liberty. And if sometimes they were obstinate and difficult
material, this very defect was perhaps an outgrowth of
their virtues. They might not have been the tower of
strength they were for the Union cause if they had not the
very defects which sometimes irritated and tried us.[10]

The Forty-Eighters, who had never learned to "play
the game" in politics, who stood simply and squarely for
their principles, did step on many an Anglo-Saxon toe. Especially the radicals stirred up controversies by bluntly stating
what was wrong in the United States.

Thus the Louisville Platform of 1854, adopted and signed
by such radicals as Burgeler, Stein, L. Wittig, B. Domschke
and C. Heinzen, begins as follows:

Liberty, prosperity and education ... have become the
privilege of classes and races who control the legislature
and administration of our country.... Peoples are over-
ruled by parties, parties governed by cliques, persons taking the place of principles and names are substituted for
rights.... This thing must be stopped.[11]

The leading firebrand behind this platform was Charles
Heinzen, of whom Horace Greeley said:

> Of all the exiles whom the European revolution brought
> to our shores none wields so trenchant, merciless, and in-
> dependent a pen as Mr. Charles Heinzen . . . he necessarily
> often shocks the feelings of his readers and makes foes
> where he might make friends, but he also often tells the
> truth.[12]

The Louisville Platform contained twelve points and
was addressed to "All True Republicans of the Union," pro-
posing an alliance between the liberal German element and
the progressive Americans "for the purpose of carrying into
full effect those grand principles of the Declaration of Independence."

The German *Turner,* or gymnasts, were closely linked
with the radical elements of the Forty-Eighters. Their in-
sistence on celebrating Sunday in picnic grounds and spending the day in merrymaking irritated many of their fellow
citizens. The *Turner* stated their purpose innocently enough
as, "Cultivation of rational training both physical and intellectual, in order that members may become energetic, patriotic citizens of the Republic, who could and would represent and protect common human liberty by word and
deed." Although their liberal, humanistic principles did not
differ drastically from those laid down by Washington,
Franklin, and Jefferson, the members of the *Turner* were
nevertheless considered a threat to the Constitution at the
height of nativism.

The *Turner* movement was begun in 1811 by Friedrich
Ludwig Jahn at the Hasenheide, a wooded field outside of
Berlin. He wanted to strengthen the Prussian youth in mind
and body to enable them to throw off the yoke of Napoleon,
who had conquered Prussia in 1806. The movement spread
quickly throughout Germany, taking firm roots at the universities. While the *Turner* and *Turnvator Jahn,* as he was
affectionately called, attracted suspicious attention from the
reactionary governments in Europe after the defeat of Napoleon, enthusiastic disciples of Jahn spread his idea to
other countries. Jahn's idea was in his own words, "The education of the people aims to realize the ideal of an all-around

human being, citizen, and member of society in each individual; gymnastics are one means toward a complete education of the people." The education of the common man apparently held little appeal for German princes and kings, however, because Jahn was imprisoned in 1819, where he remained for five years, and the *Turner* societies were suppressed until 1842.

Jahn's system of physical training was introduced to the United States as early as 1824 by two prominent German scholars in Massachusetts. Charles Follen was called to teach German literature at Harvard, but in 1826, after organizing a gymnasium fashioned after Jahn's model, Follen taught physical education as well. Carl Beck was teaching Latin at Round Hill School and supervised the building of the first gymnasium in the United States in 1824. Beck translated Jahn's *Deutsche Turnkunst* into English and taught physical education classes according to Jahn's system.

In 1827 another disciple of *Turnvater Jahn,* Francis Lieber, introduced gymnastic training to Boston and established a swimming school which attracted considerable attention. Lieber's program of physical education was backed enthusiastically by Dr. J. C. Warren of the Harvard Medical School.

The *Turner* movement in the United States gained nationwide attention with the arrival of the Forty-Eighters, who regarded the *Turnvereine* as another means for the advancement of their political and social ideas. In October, 1848 the first *Turngemeinde* was founded in Cincinnati. The founders were three *Turner* from Ludwigsburg and Friedrich Hecker, who persuaded his friend Kienzel, a businessman in Cincinnati, to lease a small lot suited for the performance of gymnastic exercises. When some good citizens did not look too kindly on the "outlandish" exhibition of flexing muscle, the *Turner* were forced to build a high board fence around the lot. But the membership increased in number and were able to dedicate their own hall on New Year's Day, 1850. This primitive board structure, forty by eighty feet, was probably the first *Turner Halle* in the United States. On its walls amidst the decorations, the motto of the *Turner* was proudly displayed: *"Frisch, fromm, froh, frei"* (alert, devout, happy, free).

Soon afterwards, *Turner* societies were organized in major cities all over the United States. By 1865 the organization had 5,995 members and eighty-two societies. The activities of the *Turner* met first with hostility, then gradually won the acceptance of their fellow citizens. The situation in Illinois as described by Professor Arthur C. Cole serves as an example:

> The tendency toward democratic Sunday amusement gained headway in the towns and cities. This was especially true of the German element which in the summer months repaired to nearby picnic grounds or Sunday gardens and spent the day in merrymaking. To the Germans of Chicago who associated the Sabbath not only with the idea of religious worship but also the festive holiday atmosphere, the gayety of their Sunday gardens at Cottage Grove or of the Holstein picnic grounds three miles out on the Milwaukee road seemed an inalienable right. On the same principle the Belleville Germans assumed certain privileges in the parades of their military company and of their "gymnastic infidel company" that annoyed their fellow-citizens. The Northwestern Sabbath Convention of 1854 therefore declared that the "vast influx of immigrants joining us from the foreign and despotic countries, who have learned in their native land to hate established religion and the Sabbath law as part of it, calls on us for special prayer and labor on behalf of this portion of our population, to reclaim them from this fatal error." Such reclamation, however, made little progress; the socially-minded westerner, indeed, found an appeal in this new gospel of the joy of life that could not be offset by his own evangels. When, therefore, the German's right to his peculiar form of Sunday observance was threatened, sturdy champions among the native elements of the population came to his aid.[13]

On the other hand, the *Turner* had some violent clashes with the once-secret political organization of the Know-

Nothing party, an influential group of nativists who never confessed to any wrongdoing by claiming to "know nothing." Among other things the Know-Nothing party was against the voting rights of naturalized citizens, a right the politically active *Turner* cherished and protected. Fights on election day were not infrequent, and were sometimes violent, as in the mayoral election of 1856, in Baltimore:

> The election took place on October 8, 1856, the candidates being Thomas Swann, Know-Nothing, and Thomas Clinton Wright, Democrat. It was attended by bloodshed and disorder wholly unprecedented in the annals of this or any other American city. In the vicinity of Lexington Market, and in the public squares surrounding the Washington monument, pitched battles were fought, in which muskets were used freely, and cannon even brought into the streets —which the authorities made no attempt to quell as they had made no provisions to prevent—which lasted without interruption for hours and finally only terminated with nightfall, and in which actually more men were killed than fell on the American side on the field of Palo Alto. The result of the election, if it may so be called, was the almost entire disenfranchisement of all naturalized citizens who were nearly driven from the polls, and the consequent elevation of Mr. Swann to the mayorality by a majority of 1,567 votes.[14]

A year before the Baltimore election incident, the *Turner* societies had entered practical politics by adopting the following platform at their National Convention in September 1855 in Buffalo, New York:

> The *Turnerbund* states that slavery, nativism and prohibition are the worst abuses of the time and in full realization of this fact sets up the following principles:
> 1) The *Turner* will vote for no man who is a member of the Know-Nothing party, or who is identified with any nativistic organization or party, or who does not declare himself openly as opposed to any organization of this nature.
> 2) The *Turner* are opposed to slavery; particularly they

are against extension of slavery to the free territories, and
regard this institution as definitely unworthy of a republic
and contrary to all concepts of freedom.

3) The *Turner* are opposed to all prohibition laws as un-
democratic and unjust in theory and not feasible in
practice.[15]

Even though this platform caused the secession of the
Turner societies in Charleston, Savannah, Mobile, and Augusta, most *Turner* groups kept its principles and were ready
to fight for them.

When President Lincoln was inaugurated, March 4, 1861,
two *Turner* companies from Washington and Baltimore
formed part of his bodyguard. The *Turner* were among the
first to respond to Lincoln's call to arms, and their outstanding contribution to the victory of the Union helped to win
them a place in American society. After the Civil War most
former critics of the *Turner* kept silent and grew accustomed
to their "outlandish" way of life.

If it is true that democracy needs its radicals lest it fall
into complacency, the Forty-Eighters and the *Turner* societies contributed their fair share of radical dreamers to
upset the complacency of their fellow citizens. Many of their
dreams were never realized, because they did not know how
to apply their ideas to the situations in the United States
which were different from those in Europe. But many others,
such as the ideals of political freedom, universal suffrage, the
importance of physical health contributed in large measure
to American values and practices.

10
Carl Schurz
and Francis Lieber

In contrast to most other Forty-Eighters, Carl Schurz was able to remain actively faithful to his principles and ideals during his successful career in American politics. When someone asked him why he insisted on striving for ideals which were as "distant as the stars," he simply replied, "The stars are what we must sail by." He found strength in his belief that American democracy is basically sound in spite of its many incongruities. To a friend in Germany he wrote, "The abuse of the good does not tempt an American to abolish it. The abuse of liberty does not tempt him to curtail liberty."

Carl Schurz was born on March 2, 1829, at Liblar not far away from Cologne. He received a good education at a Catholic high school at Cologne and at the age of eighteen entered the University of Bonn. There he fell under the spell of Gottfried Kinkel, a young professor who favored the cause of the revolution in Germany as "a united and more democratic government." Toward the end of February 1848, Louis Phillipe was dethroned in France and revolutionary uprisings occurred in Germany. The Prussian army, however, soon had everything under control; Professor Kinkel was imprisoned and Schurz had to flee the country. But Schurz returned to rescue his beloved professor from prison. Risking his own life, Schurz succeeded and fled with Kinkel to England. Although barely twenty-one, Schurz became a celebrity in Europe and was compared to other famous European revolutionaries, Kossuth and Mazzini, for his bravery.

Schurz waited in England for a turn of events in Germany. But late in 1851, when Louis Napoleon regained his throne, hopes for political changes in Germany dwindled also. In this situation, as Schurz noted later in his *Reminiscences*:

> The fatherland was closed to me. England was to me a foreign country, and would always remain so. Where, then? "To America," I said to myself.... *Ubi libertas, ibi patria*—I formed my resolution on the spot. I would remain only a short time longer in England to make some necessary preparations, and then—off to America.[1]

At that time Schurz was visiting a wealthy German exile in England, who introduced Schurz to Margaretha Meyer, daughter of a wealthy Hamburg merchant. Schurz later described her as "a girl of about eighteen years ... of fine stature, a curly head, something childlike in her beautiful features and large, dark, truthful eyes." They fell in love with each other at first sight. Margaretha agreed to go with him to America. They were married in London in 1852 and left soon afterwards for New York, where they were delightfully startled at the absence of authority," no military sentinels at public buildings; no soldiers on the streets ... no uniformed official except the police."

The Schurzes settled down in Watertown, Wisconsin, where Mrs. Schurz opened the first kindergarten, thus making a lasting contribution to American education. With keen interest Carl Schurz studied American political institutions, prepared for a law career, and was admitted to the bar in 1858. In Washington he was received by Jefferson Davis, Secretary of War, and Senator Shields of Illinois who, as Schurz noted, "welcomed me with effective cordiality as a sort of fellow revolutionary—he himself, as an enthusiastic

Irish nationalist, being in a state of permanent belligerency against England."

Carl Schurz was very much impressed by his adopted country. He wrote in one of his letters:

> Here in America you can see every day how little a people needs to be governed. There are governments, but no masters; there are governors, but they are only commissioners, agents. There are great institutions, the lines of communication, etc., almost always owe their existence not to official authority but to the spontaneous cooperation of private citizens. Here you witness the productiveness of freedom. You see a magnificent church—a voluntary association of private persons has founded it; an orphan asylum built of marble—a wealthy citizen has erected it; a university—some rich men have left a large bequest for educational purposes, which serves as a capital stock, and the university then lives, so to speak, almost on subscriptions; and so on without end. We learn here how superfluous is the action of governments concerning a multitude of things in which in Europe it is deemed absolutely indispensable, and how the freedom to do something awakens the desire to do it.[2]

Schurz early associated himself with the Republican party, helping to organize the party in Wisconsin, and becoming its nominee for lieutenant governor in 1856. Though he lost the election, he won the respect of his fellow Republicans. In 1860 he led the Wisconsin delegation to the Republican National Convention in Chicago, which favored Seward's nomination through the last ballot. There was no antagonism towards Lincoln, as Schurz remarked later, "He was universally recognized as a true antislavery leader who had done our cause very great service. We esteemed him most highly, but we did not favor his nomination because we were for Seward 'first, last, and all the time.' "[3]

When Lincoln won the nomination, it was not difficult for Schurz to support him, and he campaigned loyally and vigorously for Lincoln. His efforts were rewarded by his appointment as United States minister to Spain. Schurz would rather have stayed in the United States to fight in the

Union army. He did not particularly like his stay in Spain, and he wrote home:

> Great titles are as common as blackberries here; but there is ordinarily little behind them. . . . I cannot endure people who abase themselves as they do here; and I am embarrassed when all manner of honors and reverences are hurled at my head. Nowhere can I feel right save in a country where people stand erect in their boots.[4]

Nevertheless, Schurz took his assignment seriously. With rare insight and statesmanship he sensed clearly that the danger of having the Confederacy recognized by the European powers was greater than believed in the United States, and that the abolition of slavery was the main objective of the Civil War. Secretary of State Seward was not convinced and did not seem willing to transmit Schurz's concern to the president. For that reason Schurz went back to Washington in 1862 to see Lincoln in person. He obtained Lincoln's consent to sound out public opinion. After weeks of inquiries Schurz was sure that the time was ripe to come out openly in favor of emancipation. On March 6, 1862, Schurz delivered a speech on behalf of abolition of slavery in the great hall of Cooper Union in New York City. Lincoln reacted by requesting of Congress a joint resolution concerning the gradual abolition of slavery in the United States. The adoption of this policy stamped the war clearly as a war against slavery and gave the antislavery forces in Europe the upper hand in support of the Union cause. Schurz, statesman at the age of thirty-three, had read the signs of the time correctly.

Schurz did not return to his post in Spain, but entered the Union army as brigadier general commanding a division in Franz Sigel's corps. One of Schurz's regimental commanders was Colonel Alexander von Schimmelpfenning, who had been Schurz's superior during the unsuccessful war in Germany. Schurz admitted openly his indebtedness to his former superior, while Schimmelpfenning complimented Schurz after the first divisional maneuvers saying, "You have studied well; now let us do as well when the bullets whistle." Though he was denounced by some as a "political general" or "civilian general," Schurz served creditably well and was promoted to major general after his troops distinguished themselves under his leadership at the battle of Lookout Mountain.

In 1864 Schurz took a leave of absence from the army, to campaign for President Lincoln's re-election. He campaigned very hard because he thoroughly believed in Lincoln, as he expressed in a letter to a friend, on October 12, 1864, "I will make a prophecy that may now sound peculiar. In fifty years, perhaps much sooner, Lincoln's name will be inscribed close to Washington's on this American Republic's roll of honor. And there it will remain for all time. The children of those who persecute him now will bless him." And there were some even in his own party who "persecuted" Lincoln during the time of re-election, as the president himself confided to Schurz:

> They urge me with almost violent language to withdraw from the contest . . . in order to make room for a better man. I wish I could. . . . Perhaps some other man might do this business better than I. . . . But I am here, and that better man is not here. . . . God knows, I have at least tried very hard to do my duty—to do right to everybody and wrong to nobody. And now to have it said . . . that I have been seduced by what they call the lust of power, and that I have been doing this and that unscrupulous thing hurtful to the common cause, only to keep myself in office! Have they thought of that common cause when trying to break me down? I hope they have.[5]

Schurz recorded this private conversation observing that "Lincoln's eyes were moist" and "his rugged features working strangely." Yet, he was able to cheer up the president by assuring him that "the people, undisturbed by the bickerings of his critics, believed in him."

Lincoln was re-elected though many people were dissatisfied with the conservative course he took in the war. Among those people were some radical Germans in Cleveland, who in 1863 proposed Fremont for president. But Lincoln remained steadfastly in office, until five days after General Lee had signed the surrender on April 14, 1865, when the president was assassinated. Vice-President Johnson then became president, and barely avoided impeachment later. He was not favored by Schurz, who was one of those who had originally received the news of Johnson's candidacy for vice-president with "a certain uneasiness of feeling." In spite of this Schurz accepted an important commission from President Johnson in the summer of 1865 to tour the Gulf States and to report on the condition of the country and the state of public opinion. In the Gulf States Schurz was told over and over again, "The Negro will not work without physical compulsion. He is lazy. He is improvident. He is inconstant. We want steady, continuous work, work that can be depended upon." His personal observations, however, caused him to believe that "the success of Negro free labor would depend not only on the aptitudes of the laborer, but also on those of the employer." Schurz's report was filled with suggestions which President Johnson chose to ignore. With Lincoln's death, Schurz's role in Washington had died as well, and he returned to journalism.

After he had worked for some time under Horace Greeley on the *New York Tribune* and as editor of the *Detroit Post,* he moved in 1867 to St. Louis to take charge of the German daily newspaper, *Die Westliche Post.* But he could not stay away long from active politics. At the Republican convention of 1868 he served as temporary chairman, making his influence count by inserting in the platform a resolution recommending a general amnesty for the South. Five years earlier he had already told the Cooper Union audience, "The best revenge for the past is that which furnishes us the best assurance for the future." This principle was followed by the United States in the wars to come and greatly benefitted defeated Germany after World Wars I and II.

Two days after his fortieth birthday, on March 4, 1869, Carl Schurz took the oath of office in the Senate of the United States. He was the first German-born citizen to become a member of the upper house of Congress. "The ambition to do something can be boundless, but it must free itself from the ambition to be something," Schurz had once written to an old friend. In this spirit he recorded in his *Reminiscences* his reflections on the first day in the Senate:

> I remember vividly the feelings which almost oppressed me. . . . Now I had actually reached the most exalted public position. . . . Little more than sixteen years had elapsed since I had landed on these shores, a homeless waif. . . . And here I was now, a member of the highest law-making body of the greatest of republics. Should I ever be able . . . to justify the honors that had been heaped upon me? To accomplish this, my conception of duty could not be pitched too high. I recorded a vow in my own heart that I would at least honestly endeavor to fulfill that duty; that I would conscientiously adhere to that principle *salus populi suprema lex;* that I would never be a sycophant of power nor a flatterer of the multitude; that, if need be, I would stand up alone for my conviction of truth and right.[6]

Following his principles rather than the party line, Schurz became more and more disenchanted with the ineptitude and corruption of the Grant administration. In 1870 Schurz and Horace Greeley organized the Liberal Republican party, to provide an alternative to Grant in the national election of 1872. When Greeley lost to Grant by a landslide, Schurz left the Republican party to establish himself as an Independent. For years to come, Schurz was the outstanding leader of the Independents. In 1875, after six years of service, he retired from the Senate, a move which James Russell Lowell called "a national misfortune."

In the presidential campaign of 1876 Schurz swayed a large independent vote to help Rutherford B. Hayes win the presidency. Hayes seemed to Schurz to be the safer man, for sound money and civil service reform. As secretary of the interior in Hayes' cabinet, Schurz had the opportunity for the first time to carry out the idea of civil service reform. He immediately announced that no one in his department would be removed except for cause, and that no promotions would be made except for merit. Claude M. Fuess, Schurz's biographer, writes:

> Schurz's most definite contribution to his adopted country was doubtless through his promotion of civil service reform ... the rapid adoption of the merit system by successive presidents was probably due more to him than any other man. In achieving his aims, he employed every legitimate device; he threatened, he bargained, he persuaded, he pleaded, he argued.... No matter what else was going on, Schurz had always a watchful eye for government appointments and seldom let a poor one slip by without protesting to the person responsible for it.[7]

To clean up the corruption within the Indian Bureau under his jurisdiction, Schurz appointed a commission. Its report of 1878 accused the Indian Bureau of "cupidity, inefficiency and the most barefaced dishonesty, ... a reproach to the whole nation." Schurz promptly reorganized the whole department by discharging the inefficient and corrupt elements. After a tour of inspection lasting for six weeks, which started in August of 1879, Schurz came out with a positive program of training young Indians. An industrial school which later came to be known as Carlisle Institute was opened for that purpose, to be followed by other schools at Chilocco, Haskell, and elsewhere. This policy did not win him any friends in the War Department, which promptly tried to take over the affairs of the Indian Bureau.

Schurz made powerful enemies for himself by formulating a conservation policy of forests and lands, curtailing the profits of the ruthless, industrial profiteers. He was the first high government official to propose such legislation to protect the natural heritage of the people and preserve it for future generations. In 1881 his term as secretary of the interior was over, and he left Hayes' cabinet, never to hold public office again.

Until the end of his life Schurz maintained interest in politics. He played an important role in the election of Grover Cleveland, Democratic presidential candidate of 1884, who had proposed to continue the practice of the civil service system as instituted by Schurz. A nonpartisan movement on Cleveland's behalf was led by Schurz, and probably won the election for Cleveland. As president, Cleveland kept his promise. His party had been out of power nationally for almost a quarter of a century and was eager for the spoils of victory, which would have been theirs, had Cleveland allowed patronage to prevail.

In 1899 at the age of seventy Schurz delivered one of his more memorable speeches at a University of Chicago convocation. The issue was American imperialism and the Philippine insurrection. Schurz was against the former, and in theory supported the latter, as the following excerpt shows:

> It is objected that they are not capable of independent government. They may answer that this is their affair and that they are at least entitled to a trial. I frankly admit that if they are given the trial, their conduct in governing themselves will be far from perfect. Well, the conduct of no people is perfect, not even our own. They may try to revenge themselves upon their Tories in their Revolutionary War. But we too threw our Tories in hideous dungeons. . . . We, too, have had our civil war which cost hundreds and thousands of lives and devastated one-half of our land; and now we have in horrible abundance the killings by lynch law. . . . They may have troubles with their wild tribes. So had we, and we treated our wild tribes in a manner not to be proud of. They may have corruption and rapacity in their government . . . but Manila may secure a city council not much less virtuous than that of Chicago.[8]

Though remaining interested in politics, Schurz devoted most of his later life to literary work. From 1881 to 1883 he was an editor of the *New York Evening Post,* and later became chief editorial writer of *Harper's Weekly.* In 1887 he published his two-volume biography of Henry Clay and completed three volumes of his *Reminiscences,* concluding with the end of the Civil War.

Schurz died in 1906 at the age of seventy-seven. On

November 21, 1906, a memorial service was convened in his
honor in New York City. Joseph H. Choate, ambassador to
England, presided over the meeting and gave the introduc-
tory address. Other speakers included former President
Cleveland, President Eliot of Harvard, Professor Eugen
Kuehnemann of Breslau, representing the German universities, Secretary of the Navy Charles J. Bonaparte, Booker
T. Washington, and editor and poet Richard Watson Gilder.
Of the many tributes paid to Schurz, the one by Mark Twain,
printed in *Harper's Weekly*, May 26, 1906, is one of the most
eloquent:

> We all realize that the release of Carl Schurz is a heavy
> loss to the country; some of us realize that it is a heavy loss
> to us individually and personally. As a rule I have a suf-
> ficiency of confidence—perhaps over-confidence—in my
> ability to hunt out the right man and sure political channel
> for myself, and follow it to the deep water beyond the reef
> without getting aground; but there have been times, in
> the past thirty years, when I lacked that confidence—
> then I dropped into Carl Schurz's wake, saying to myself,
> "he is as safe as Ben Thornburgh." When I was a young
> pilot on the Mississippi nearly half a century ago, the fel-
> lowship numbered among its masters three incomparables:
> Horace Bixby, Beck Jolly, and Ben Thornburgh. Where
> they were not afraid to venture with a steamboat, the rest
> of the guild were not afraid to follow. Yet there was a dif-
> ference: of the three, they preferred to follow Thornburgh;
> for sometimes the other two depended on native genius
> and almost inspirational water-reading to pick out the
> lowest place on the reef, but that was not Ben Thornburgh's
> way; if there were serious doubts he would stop the
> steamer and man the sounding-barge and go down and
> sound the several crossings and lay buoys upon them.
> Nobody needed to search for the best water after Ben
> Thornburgh. If he could not find it no one could. I felt
> that way about him; and so, more than once I waited for
> him to find the way, then dropped into his steamer's wake
> and ran over the wrecks of his buoys on half steam until
> the leadsman's welcome cry of "mark twain" informed me
> that I was over the bar all right, and could draw a full
> breath again.

I had this same confidence in Carl Schurz as a political channel finder. I had the highest opinion of his inborn qualifications for the office: his blemishless honor, his unassailable patriotism, his high intelligence, his penetration; I also had the highest opinion of his acquired qualifications as a channel finder. I believed he could read the political surfaces as accurately as Bixby could read the faint and fleeting signs upon Mississippi's face— the pretty dimple that hid a deadly rock, the ostentatious wind-reef that had nothing under it, the sleek and inviting dead stretch that promised quarter-less-twain and couldn't furnish six feet. And—more than all—he was my Ben Thornburgh in this: whenever he struck out a new course over a confused Helena Reach or a perplexed Plum Point Bend I was confident that he had not contented himself with reading the water, but had hoisted out his sounding-barge and buoyed that maze from one end to the other. Then I dropped into his wake and followed. Followed with perfect confidence. Followed, and never regretted it.

I have held him in the sincerest affection, esteem, and admiration for more than a generation. I have not always sailed with him politically, but whenever I have doubted my own competency to choose the right course, I have struck my two-taps-and-one ("get out the port and starboard lead"), and followed him through without doubt or hesitancy. By and by I shall wish to talk of Carl Schurz, the man and friend, but not now; at this time I desire only to offer this brief word of homage and reverence to him, as from a grateful pupil in citizenship to the master who is no more.[9]

Carl Schurz led the fight against slavery in the Middle West. As general in the Civil War he served the cause of the Union and not his own interests. By his own example he made the Civil Service Reform work, and as secretary of the interior fought corruption in the federal government and proved himself a true friend of the Indians. Carl Schurz was the champion of any liberal cause between the Civil War and the turn of the century. He raised his voice loud and clear to bring about a conservation program protecting American soil and forests from greedy exploit, no matter how many enemies he made. Six years before his death he warned against American imperialism at a time when most political voices clamored for another "manifest destiny" beyond the American shores. His military as well as his civil courage was of a special kind. In the words of Allan Nevins, "Courage is not a rare virtue; but the resolutely independent and discriminating courage of a Schurz, which made him ready in the name of principle to face any public clamor, and to turn against an old friend almost as quickly as against an old foe, is rare indeed."

Claude M. Fuess sizes up Carl Schurz rather well in his book *Carl Schurz, Reformer,*

> For forty years or more he was the self-constituted but exceedingly useful, incarnation of our national conscience. ... Historians have been forced to admit that he was right on most issues; and even when he was wrong, he was sincere. Naturally he did not make himself popular, but he did, without being at all sanctimonious, become a mighty spiritual force.[10]

*   *   *   *   *

Next to Carl Schurz, perhaps the most serious-minded of the many firebrands and radicals of the Forty-Eighters was Francis Lieber. Born in Berlin in 1800, he came to the United States in 1827 after an interesting odyssey through Europe. When Lieber was fifteen, Napoleon had escaped from Elba to take his last stand on European battlefields. In spite of his youth, Lieber enlisted in the veteran Pomeranian Colberg regiment and fought against Napoleon in the fierce battles of Ligny and Waterloo. In the attack on Namur he was severely wounded. After his recovery he returned to Berlin to finish his studies at high school and at the University of Berlin, where he was expelled for his liberal political views. He then went to the University of Jena, where he earned his Ph.D. in 1820. Being a soldier at heart he went to Greece to fight for the cause of freedom in 1821. The Greeks were trying to shake off Turkish rule, but it was not until 1830 that they won their independence with the help of England, France, and Russia. After many hardships

Lieber left Greece for Italy in 1822. After paying his sea passage all the money left to him was one and one-half scudi, approximately equal in value to a dollar and a half. He made his way to Rome on foot, where he applied for help at the Prussian embassy. Fortunately, George Niebuhr, the famous historian of ancient Rome, was the ambassador at that time. He took pity on the penniless Lieber and kept him for a year in his household as a tutor for his oldest son. Through his political influence Niebuhr gained permission for Lieber to return to Berlin. In spite of the influence of his well-meaning protector, however, Lieber was thrown into prison upon arrival. Only after much trouble and red tape did Niebuhr succeed in getting Lieber released. The reactionary forces in Germany were so strong that Lieber could be safe only in exile. In 1825 he left for London where he supported himself by tutoring and newspaper work.

In 1827 Lieber's fortunes changed for the better. He arrived in Boston with references from Niebuhr which opened many an influential door. As mentioned earlier, he accepted a position as an instructor of gymnastics and had the support of Dr. J. C. Warren of the Harvard Medical School. More importantly he started the literary career in which he gradually won international renown as a scholar. With the assistance of his friend Judge Story, and G. S. Hillard of Boston, he started an adaptation of the Brockhaus *Konversations-Lexicon,* a work which was called the *Encyclopaedia Americana,* forming the basis for the subsequent *American Encyclopedia.* Lieber's articles on political science and on Greece, and his biographies of Grotius, Machiavelli, and Montesquieu attracted the attention of Boston's elite. During his six-year stay in Boston he counted among his friends Josiah Quincy, president of Harvard University, the historians William Hickling Prescott and George Bancroft, and later, John Lothrop Motley, George Ticknor, Charles Sumner, and poet Henry Wadsworth Longfellow.

In 1833 he was called to Philadelphia to draw up a plan for the education of the students of Girard College. While in Philadelphia he won the friendship of such important men as banker H. C. Carey, jurists Binney and C. J. Ingersoll,

Judge Thayer, and ex-King of Spain Joseph Bonaparte. In
1835, South Carolina College, Columbia, S. C., offered him a
professorship of history and political economy. Lieber accepted and found the time to write works which made him
famous as a scholar of international law: *Manual of Political
Ethics* (1837), *Legal and Political Hermeneutics* (1839), and
Civil Liberty and Self-Government (1853). "These works,"
writes Judge Thayer, "are all written with as much ease and
purity of idiom as if English had been his native language,
a fact not more remarkable than that he, a German, should
have become the great American teacher of the Philosophy
of Anglican Political Science."

In 1856 Lieber went to Columbia College, New York,
to teach political science in the law department. During the
Civil War he advised President Lincoln on important ques-
tions of military and international law. The president and
General Halleck requisitioned him to write on the "Code of
War for the Government and the Armies of the United
States in the Field." This code was adopted by the army of
the North and published as *General Order #100 of the War
Department.* Two of Lieber's sons, Hamilton and Norman,
fought in the Union army. His oldest son, Oscar, who had
married a Southern girl, joined Wade Hampton's legion in
South Carolina, and died in the battle of Williamsburg.

Francis Lieber died October 2, 1872. His life-long motto
had been *"Patria cara, carior libertas, veritas carissima"*—
his country was dear to him, liberty dearer, but dearest of
all was truth. A letter Lieber wrote shortly before his death
on August 11, 1872, to Franz von Holzendorff has endeared
him to many immigrants:

> I do not agree with you in what you say about modern
> emigration. At all times men have looked for a better coun-
> try, when the country of their birth became too crowded
> or too barren, and our easy mode of transportation has
> naturally brought about a new and peaceful migration.
> To possess a portion of the earth, to call a few acres his
> own, to one who has for years cultivated fields that belong
> to others, and who perhaps could eat meat but fifteen times
> during the year. You should see the Swedes in Minnesota

or the Germans in Missouri or Kansas, where they point
to their one hundred and fifty or two hundred acres of land.
The right to emigrate belongs to the earliest right of the
individual. Through emigration the Almighty has directed
mankind to spread over the earth; and the higher and more
uniform the culture, the more emigration and immigration
will increase. The emigrant by no means proves that he
has no love for his country, especially if a man who would
have gladly sacrificed himself for his fatherland has been
forced from it, as in times past.[11]

Many other individuals among the group of the German
Forty-Eighters made their marks on American history. As
an indication of this, the *Dictionary of American Biography*
includes entries for one hundred and three persons born
in Germany or Austria for the period 1846-1855, while for
the entire eighteenth century, only fifty-seven immigrants
from Germany and Austria were considered worthy to be
included.

11
Political Activism

Cartoonist Thomas Nast was a politician—though only with his pen. He was born in 1840, at Landau, in the Bavarian Palatinate and emigrated to New York when he was six years of age. His father was a musician and, though highly skilled and a member of the Philharmonic Society of New York, he could provide only a meager existence for his family. Thomas attended evening classes at the Academy of Design, and while still a teenager was hired as an illustrator by Frank Leslie, publisher of *Leslie's Weekly*. In 1860 when Nast was only twenty years old, *The New York Illustrated News* sent him to England to sketch the Heenan-Sayers prize-fight. From there he went to Italy and participated in the Sicilian War of Liberation under Garibaldi. His sketches of the Italian war appeared in European and American newspapers. When he returned to New York in 1861 his great period as a political caricaturist began. From 1862 to 1866 he was staff artist for *Harper's Weekly*. Near the close of the Civil War, Abraham Lincoln said of him, "Thomas Nast has been our best recruiting sergeant; his emblematic cartoons have never failed to arouse enthusiasm and patriotism, and have always seemed to come just when these articles were getting scarce."[1]

In the 1870s Nast's pen helped to rid New York City of the Tweed Ring of the Tammany organization. The Republican elephant appeared first in his cartoon, "The Third Term Panic." Most of Nast's cartoons appeared in *Harper's Weekly,* whose owner, J. Henry Harper, paid him the finest tribute:

> Nast was one of the great statesmen of his time. I have never known a man with a surer political insight. He seemed to see approaching events before most men dreamed them as possible. His work was entirely his own and generally in his own way. He never could bear interference or even suggestion. I never knew him to use an idea that was not his own.[2]

Though nineteenth century German-Americans were often politically active, many earlier German immigrants did not show much interest in politics or in holding public office. In December 1694, when Paul Wulff was elected clerk of Germantown, Pennsylvania, he declined to serve and was fined three pounds by the General Court for refusing the office without good cause. In 1703 Pastorius wrote to William Penn complaining how difficult it was to get his Germans to serve as public officers. Notwithstanding the deep mistrust many a German seems to have toward politics—there is an old German proverb that "politics spoils the character"—future generations of German immigrants served their adopted country well in the political arena. The influence of the German Forty-Eighters on American politics remains unquestioned, and the involvement of men and women of German stock in contemporary politics is apparent and notable.

One of the foremost troubleshooters in today's turbulent political world has been Henry Kissinger. On September 22, 1973, he was sworn in as the fifty-sixth secretary of state, the first naturalized citizen to be appointed to this honorable position. Deeply moved, Kissinger stated after the ceremony, as quoted in Marvin and Bernard Kalb's book on Kissinger: "There is no country in the world where it is conceivable that a man of my origin could be standing here next to the President of the United States."[3] When he was thirteen years old, he and his family were forced out of Nazi Germany. As an adult in this country, his phenomenal rise from Harvard professor to the position of secretary of state is well known. His services to the United States and the world as a mediator of conflicts which threatened world peace have been unsurpassed in modern history.

During the recent Watergate scandal several persons of German descent played an important but less honorable role. This induced some people to speak of a "German Mafia" surrounding President Nixon. This label was not only unfair but totally inaccurate. There simply was no relationship between the men of German descent who were involved in Watergate which could be described as "Mafia-like."

Others of German descent who played important roles "on the other side" of the Watergate investigations, such as former Secretary of the Treasury Shultz, as well as the many members of the various congressional committees investigating Watergate would resent the implications of the use of the label of "German Mafia." One outstanding member of this group was Senator Lowell P. Weicker Jr., outspoken member of the Senate Watergate Committee. The senator's grandfather arrived in the United States about 1890 from Darmstadt, Germany. As a chemist with a degree from Heidelberg University, grandfather Weicker teamed up with Dr. Edward Robinson Squibb, a pharmacist in Brooklyn, to set up what was to become one of the most profitable pharmaceutical businesses in the United States. He died in 1940. His grandson Lowell (at six feet, six inches, the tallest member of the United States Senate), has been a champion of Republican interest in political life and in fact prompted immediate applause from the spectators in the Senate Caucus Room when he stated on June 28, 1973, that "Republicans do not cover up . . . do not threaten, do not commit illegal acts. And God knows, Republicans don't view their opponents as enemies to be harassed." Moreover, he has made public statements to set the issue of loyalty straight. In an interview with Lloyd Shearer, as reported in *Parade* magazine July 14, 1974, the senator was particularly vexed about the equation of "disagreement equals disloyalty." "Such logic," he said, "reflects the attitude of the Nixon administration, which sought to 'get' the guys who disagreed with their policies." By declining an invitation to a "Peace with Honor" reception at the White House, Senator Weicker made clear that he did not share this kind of logic. He told his interviewer, "Last year in February, I was invited to the White House for a 'Peace with Honor' reception. I learned that invitations were extended, not to the whole Congress in celebration of getting us out of Vietnam, but only those of us who had supported the president's position. Since the reception was designated 'Peace with Honor,' the implication was clear—those who had disagreed either did not want peace or they were dishonorable men and women. Apparently it never occurred to the White House that people who doubted the correctness of our role in Vietnam were just as patriotic and helpful in getting us out of the quagmire as were the President and his supporters."

Certainly it is a fact that several of those involved in the responsibility for Watergate are of German descent, and it is just as true that many hundreds and thousands of other Americans of German descent are successfully and honorably involved in American political life, and along with Senator Weicker believe that "the major lesson of Watergate is that we can not live with government agencies that are influenced or pressured to impose conformity of thought and action upon the people of this country by equating dissent with disloyalty."

12
Musical Traditions

From colonial times to the present, the influence of German-American singers and musicians on the quality and atmosphere of American life has been tremendous. The Quakers of Philadelphia and the Puritans of New England shared a religious distrust of music, but an impetus toward a more joyful life was given during colonial times by male and female choirs like those of the Ephrata cloister in Pennsylvania and by such vocal and instrumental music as that of the Moravians at Bethlehem, Pennsylvania, and their other settlements.

The Ephrata community, not far from Philadelphia on the Cocalico River, had been founded by the German sectarian Conrad Beissel. He had gathered there three hundred followers, men and women, to share with him a cloistered life. They had built a house for the brethren, Bethany, and a house for the sisters, Saron. Celibacy was not strictly prescribed but preferred. Married couples built their own huts close to the cloister, but all members shared their property. They celebrated Saturday instead of Sunday as the day of rest and prayer. Vegetables and spring water were their food and drink. They slept in small cells on wooden benches with a wooden block as a pillow. Following the custom of Catholic monastics, Conrad Beissel changed the civilian names of his believers. He called himself Friedsam, "the peaceful one."

Their austere way of life was elevated by the singing of hymns in their religious services. Beissel had his own system of harmony which violated all recognized musical rules up to that time. In their hymns and songs, written and composed by the prior Friedsam and other brethren, they tried to imitate the sound of the Aeolean harp. Actually the choir sang in a falsetto voice, with the lips half open. The singing of the sisters in particular seemed to come from instruments, and the choir of the Ephrata community was famous and admired in its time. Contemporary listeners commented on "the peculiar sweetness and weird beauty of the songs of the sisterhood," and "the impressive cadence of the chorals and hymns of the combined choirs." Some even remarked on the "angelic or celestial quality of the vocal music as it floated through the spaces of the large *Saal,* as the responses were sung and reverberated from the gallery to choir."[1]

The United Brethren (Moravians) established the first regular music schools in America. Their love for music and singing had a lasting influence on religious life in America. The Wesley brothers, founders of Methodism, were particularly impressed. John Wesley borrowed both themes and melodies from the Moravian hymn book to further the purposes of the Methodist religious service. When President Washington visited the settlements of the Brethren in North Carolina, he was greeted by "several melodies . . . partly by trumpets and French horns, partly by trombones." The traditional Easter sunrise service of the United Brethren in Winston-Salem and Bethlehem, celebrated with elaborate music bands playing old chorals, still attracts thousands of listeners today.

The formation of musical societies was a step forward in the development of music in America. Several musicians from Hamburg, Germany, formed a band as early as 1783 in Philadelphia. The German Gottlieb Graupner was one of the leading figures in founding the Handel and Haydn

Society at Boston in 1815. The Musical Fund Society of Philadelphia, begun in 1820, arranged both sacred and secular
programs and combined instrumental and vocal music at its
concerts.

The Philharmonic Society of New York gave its first
concert in December 1842. Its founder Uriah C. Hill was assisted by a German, Henry C. Timm. In his "Reminiscences,"
Timm recalls:

> The work of the society was a very uphill struggle, both
> musically and financially. I remember one season when
> after paying expenses each member received $17.50 as his
> share. It was, however, rather a labor of love than any-
> thing else, and we persevered. We had, however, in the
> course of years, a gradual acquisition of new and very
> good members coming almost exclusively from Germany,
> so that after the eighth season I gave up my trombone to
> a much better player than I was. We also engaged per-
> manent able conductors, such as Mr. Theodore Eisfeld and
> afterwards Carl Bergmann, so everything was gradually
> improved.[2]

The New York Philharmonic Society increased steadily
in numbers. Around 1890 it had ninety-four players of which
eighty-nine were Germans.

Theodore Thomas is an example of a German who made
outstanding achievements in American orchestral music.
Born in Esens, Germany, in 1835, Thomas came with his
parents to this country at the age of ten. In 1864, in New
York City, he founded his own orchestra, which became the
rival of the New York Philharmonic Society. This rivalry
was beneficial to the cause of music, forcing both organizations to do their best. In the summer of 1866 Thomas inaugurated garden concerts in New York which were successful
for a number of years. During the winter Thomas's orchestra
toured the United States. Those tours both stimulated other
cities to form orchestras and revived the efforts of existing
organizations.

Theodore Thomas went to Chicago to lead and develop
its symphony orchestra, and in 1891, he founded the Chicago

Symphony Orchestra. Fifty businessmen supported the orchestra and covered its financial expenses. Thomas was a musician who did not descend to the public's taste, but tried to force the public to come up to his. He and other musicians like him succeeded in developing the musical taste of Americans.

When Dr. Leopold Damrosch became the manager of the German Opera House in New York for the 1884-1885 season, operas by German composers began to compete well with Italian and French operas. Damrosch was born in Posen, Germany, in 1832. Following the wish of his parents, he studied medicine and received his medical degree from the University of Berlin in 1854. He then turned to the study of music and became a member of the Court Orchestra in Weimar in 1856. There he studied under Liszt, who made him a fervent disciple of the musical drama of Richard Wagner. In 1871 Damrosch came to New York. His Wagner evenings at the Met were very successful. One evening in February of 1885, Damrosch caught a severe cold after a performance of *Lohengrin* and died a few days later.

Anton Seidl, considered by many critics the ablest conductor of German opera, succeeded Damrosch at the Met. Seidl was born in Pesth (Austria-Hungary) of German stock. He was a personal friend of Wagner and had twice been conductor at Bayreuth before coming to America. Unfortunately for music lovers, Anton Seidl died suddenly in 1898.

Today, German opera is holding its place at the Met as well as in the repertoire of lyric opera companies throughout the country.

Every city with a German population has its singing societies. The Philadelphia *Maennerchor,* founded December 15, 1835, is the oldest singing society in the United States. With the advent of the Forty-Eighters and the *Turner* societies in the middle of the nineteenth century, the singing societies increased rapidly in number. A surprising number of the singing societies founded in the nineteenth century survived two world wars and the anti-German sentiments connected with them. In Chicago, for example, there are

about twenty-five choruses active today. The purposes of
the singing societies were and are both musical and social.
The spring and fall concerts are followed by dancing, meeting old friends and making new friends, and enjoying good
German-style food and drink.

There are many names in American music which would
be mainly of interest to the musical scholar and historian,
but there are two stars, Oscar Hammerstein and Madame
Schumann-Heink, whose popularity and influence have been
tremendous.

Oscar Hammerstein was born in Berlin in 1847. At the
age of seventeen he ran away from home and made his way
to New York. His first job as a cigar maker brought him
some money when he invented a machine for stripping tobacco. The American Tobacco Company bought his patent,
and Hammerstein invested the money in two German-
language theaters in New York. In 1870 he became the owner
of the Stadt Theater.

Harlem was at that time a white residential neighborhood, where Hammerstein built the Harlem Opera House
and an apartment block on Seventh Avenue between 136th
and 137th streets. The neighbors did not like it when Oscar
named his property for Kaiser Wilhelm and installed a statue
of the Kaiser on the cornice of the block-long apartment
building.

Soon, however, Hammerstein won popular acclaim by
producing vaudeville shows and musical comedies. In 1906 he
built the Manhattan Opera House, which rivalled the Metropolitan Opera. So great was the success of his competition
that the Met paid him $1.5 million when Hammerstein
agreed not to produce grand opera in New York for the next
ten years. However, his later attempt to challenge Covent
Garden in London was a failure. He soon left London snarl-
ing, "I'd rather be dead in New York than alive in London."
The name Hammerstein was to be a lively force indeed for
decades to come, on the musical stage; after Oscar's death
in 1919, it was kept alive by his sons.

Ernestine Schumann-Heink was a Viennese, the daughter of an army officer father and an Italian mother. At the

age of fifteen she signed a contract with the Royal Opera of Dresden and three years later married its secretary, Paul Heink, who subsequently deserted Ernestine and their three children. Fortunately, the Hamburg Opera employed her, where she became a great success. She then married actor Paul Schumann with whom she left for the United States in 1898.

The manager of the Metropolitan Opera who had brought her over here was somewhat stunned when he greeted a woman eight months pregnant instead of the glamourous star he had expected. "You will not be able to sing," he told her. But she retorted, "What do you know about babies? I have had them many a time. I shall sing regardless. You will see how I shall sing!"[3] And she did sing and was a great success in *Lohengrin*, her debut performance at the Met.

The baby born soon afterwards was given the name George Washington Schumann, to show Ernestine's affection for her new home country. While her oldest son, August, joined the Austrian army and was killed in one of the first battles of World War I, her four other sons served on the Allied side. During the war she spent most of her time appearing on programs in American Expeditionary Forces training camps, where she brought tears streaming down "doughboy faces" by singing Brahm's "Lullaby," "The Rosary," and "Silent Night." In postwar years, she became a radio star. Her voice was aging, but never lost its emotional depth. And it was said of her that "many another prima donna had successfully mothered a large family. But she has gone further. She has mothered audiences, mothered towns and cities, mothered the A.E.F., and now mothers the American Legion."[4]

Producer Louis B. Mayer wanted her to make a movie, and she signed a contract at the age of seventy-five—"Hollywood's oldest starlet," as she said. But in 1936, before she could become a movie star, she died in the manner she had wished—"I want to die singing, not in a manner to create a disturbance, but quietly, with a song on my lips."[5] At a time when anti-German feelings were strong in the United States, Madame Ernestine Schumann-Heink probably did more than any other person to remind Americans of the great loyalty of most German-Americans to their adopted country.

With their love for music it is not surprising that many German-Americans made a name for themselves in the manufacture of musical instruments. In the field of piano-making German-American craftsmen and firms are particularly numerous and famous. John Behrent constructed the first pianoforte made in this country in Philadelphia, in 1775. He was followed by Gutwaldt, Conrad Meyer, Sackmeister, and by many firms such as George Steck & Company, Kranich & Back, Mehlin & Sons, William Knabe & Company, and many more. The leading concert piano is the one manufactured by Steinway & Sons.

The founder of the firm, Henry Steinway (originally Steinweg), was born in 1797 in the Duchy of Brunswick. As a young man he learned the trade of a cabinet maker, and used his skill to fashion zithers and guitars. In Goslar, Germany, he learned how to build organs and pianos. He established his own piano factory in Brunswick, in 1825. Hampered by a narrow guild system, he put his factory in the care of his eldest son, Theodore, and left with his four other sons for New York to seek a fairer prospect for success. After he and his sons had served an apprenticeship, they set up their own factory in 1853, making one piano a week. Steinway made many improvements on the piano, one of which is the addition of a third pedal, which allows the pianist to hold single tones without affecting the others. The skill and energy of the Steinway family were crowned with success. When Henry Steinway died in 1871, he left a flourishing business in the capable hands of his sons.

Of the many names in the manufacture of violins, the name Georg Gemuender stands out as a pioneer in this country and as a maker of violins of the highest standard. Georg was born at Ingelfingen, Germany, in 1816. His father manufactured musical instruments, and he sent his son into the shops of the best European masters to learn the trade. For a number of years Georg was the apprentice and assistant of the greatest violin-maker of the time, Vuillaume, in Paris. Here he learned to distinguish the best works of Italian

and other European makers, and to imitate them. In his autobiography Gemuender relates an amusing story of how he
surprised the Norwegian violinist and composer Ole Bull.
On return from an American concert tour in 1845, Ole had
his famous violin, "Caspar da Salo," repaired by Vuillaume
in Paris. Vuillaume, without the knowledge of the maestro,
turned over the job to his assistant, Gemuender. Several
years later, Ole Bull was making another concert tour in
the United States and one day visited Gemuender's shop,
who in the meantime had settled in New York. Showing his
violin, Ole challenged Georg to detect the place where it
had once been repaired. Since Gemuender had repaired the
violin at Vuillaume's shop in Paris, it was easy for him to
find the spot though it could never have been detected by
anyone else. So Georg had met the challenge, and finally admitted to the surprised Ole that he, and not Vuillaume, had
fixed the violin.

Gemuender's imitations of Stradivarius, Amati, and
Guarnerius received first prize at the London Exposition of
1851. At the Vienna Exposition of 1873 Gemuender's "Kaiser
violin" received first prize for the best imitation. According
to the judges this violin was "a genuine Guarnerius not only
to its outer appearance and character, but also in the won-
derful quality of tone, and ease with which the tones come."
Georg fooled many of the greatest violin players by having
them choose between two violins, one a new violin of his
own make, and the other an old Italian instrument. In many
instances the violinist selected Gemuender's violin. No won-
der that the violins manufactured by Gemuender & Sons
rank with the best in the world.

13
Printing and Publishing

Equally as famous as the choir of the Ephrata community were the printing press and paper mill set up in 1740. The most important book coming from this press was the so-called "Martyr-Book," an account of Anabaptist martyrdoms. The Dutch original by Jans van Braght was translated into German by Peter Miller, who later succeeded Conrad Beissel as prior of the Ephrata monastery. Fifteen of the brothers worked three years on its publication. When it finally appeared in print in 1748, it contained 1,514 pages, which made it the largest book of the colonial period. Thirteen hundred books were printed and sold for twenty shillings apiece. Tragically, some of those books were confiscated by soldiers of the Revolutionary War, and the paper used to protect and clean their rifles.

Two other German-American presses made a name for themselves during colonial times. One was established by Christoph Sauer, the other by Henry Miller.

Christoph Sauer arrived in Germantown, Pennsylvania, in 1727. He had been a tailor in Germany, but became a "jack of all trades" here. He scored his greatest success as a bookprinter. The German Bible coming from his press in

1743 was the first book published in a European language in America. He also edited and printed a newspaper to which four thousand people subscribed. This was quite a success considering the time and language. When Christoph Sauer died in 1758, his son of the same name continued with the bookprinting business. The younger Sauer issued a second and third edition of the German Bible. The profit he made was so unexpected that he printed and distributed a *Spiritual Magazine* (1764) gratis. This was the first religious periodical published in America, making Sauer the founder of the religious press today.

Christoph Sauer Jr. had other talents too: he was the first type-founder of this country, originated the stoves which Benjamin Franklin improved and made famous, and he was one of the founders of the Germantown Academy which opened its doors in 1761. The Sauer family belonged to the religious sect of the Dunkards, which held many beliefs in common with the Quakers and Mennonites, such as separation of church and state, freedom of conscience, simplicity of dress, and refusal to take oaths or bear arms. Adult baptism by total immersion is one of the differences separating the Dunkards from other sects.

Christoph Sauer Jr. and his son Christopher Sauer III remained loyal to the English king during the Revolutionary War. For this reason the family's property was confiscated and sold in 1778, and the family was banned from Germantown. Christoph Sauer Jr. stayed at a friend's house nearby, supporting himself as a bookbinder and died in 1784. His sons Christopher and Peter moved to New York in 1777 following General Howe's army. Howe had taken Philadelphia on September 26, 1777, and the Sauer brothers had issued a paper meant primarily for the Hessian troops under Howe. Christopher Sauer became postmaster and printer in St. John, New Brunswick, after the war, where he published the *Royal Gazette*. In 1799 he moved to Baltimore, where his brother Samuel owned a printing shop and died there July 3, 1799. Peter Sauer became a physician and died of yellow fever in 1784 at Cat Island in the West Indies.

Henry Miller, the competitor of the younger Sauer in

the publishing business, favored the cause of the Revolution. In his youth he had worked as a printer in a great number of European cities. In 1760 he established his own press in Philadelphia and became the printer to Congress. His newspaper surpassed Sauer's in circulation and was widely read throughout the colonies. Since his paper was the only one in Philadelphia appearing on Fridays, and the Declaration of Independence was adopted on a Thursday, he claimed to have been the first one to print the news. As a matter of fact, he printed the entire document in German for Pennsylvania and other colonies.

At times there were as many as thirty-eight German papers being printed and published in the colonies. In the nineteenth century the number of German newspapers and magazines increased tremendously. Much credit for the increase must be given to the Forty-Eighters, many of whom were university trained and became spokesmen for the German-Americans through their writing. *Das Buch der Deutschen in Amerika,* edited under the auspices of the National German American Alliance at Walther's printing shop (Philadelphia, 1909, p. 592), lists 785 German papers which were published in the United States. Today the German-Americans generally do not rely on German language papers for the news. The number of German newspapers has decreased greatly, as indicated by Chicago's *Abendpost-Sonntagspost* which claims to be the only daily in the German language in the Middle West.

The length of the list of names of all German-American printers and journalists would be prohibitive to include here. But mention should be made of two men whose inventions did much for the development of printing and publishing. They are Louis Prang and Ottmar Mergenthaler.

Louis Prang came to the United States in 1850. He settled as a wood-engraver in Boston. Soon afterwards he established himself as a lithographer, color-printer, and publisher. He wrote on many subjects, foremost becoming the author of the *Prang Method of Art Instruction* and the *Prang Standard of Color.* Louis Prang was both the pioneer and the developer of the finest color-work in this country. He is also credited for introducing the Christmas card and thus may be blamed for the fact that each Christmas we have the tedious job of writing hundreds of Christmas greetings to our relatives and friends.

Ottmar Mergenthaler came to Baltimore in 1872. He facilitated the work of type-setting by his invention of the Linotype machine: "It set a line of type from its own brass matrices, which were then redistributed automatically; the lead in which the lines were cast was later thrown back into the melting pot beneath the machine to be endlessly reused."[1] The *New York Tribune* was the first to try the Linotype machine in 1886. Mergenthaler's machine revolutionized composition and type-setting in the printing industry, and provided speed and efficiency which allowed untold expansion in publication and the spread of information. Mergenthaler's machine is still used today, though it is gradually being replaced by computerized type-setting.

14
German Food and Drink

"Eating and drinking holds body and soul together" is an old German proverb, and it seems that most Germans live by it. With this in mind and eyeing the pecuniary advantages, many German-Americans went into the food business. Besides Oscar Mayer's wieners and Heinz's "57 Varieties," there are many other food products processed by German-Americans—too many to mention.

When touring the United States it is always possible to find good eating places in rural districts with large German populations. The Amana villages of Iowa provide a good example. Tourists return there again and again to enjoy a hearty meal served family-style.

Every American who can afford the price raves about the fine food products sold at the *delikatessengeschaefte*. The word "delicatessen" actually means delicate eating, delicate food. The home-made sausages offered at the several *Schlachtfeste* of different German-American organizations are another unforgettable, enjoyable treat for anyone who has ever sampled them.

Christmas for the German housewife is a busy time of baking all the traditional goodies, according to time-honored recipes. Herman Hagedorn recalls in his book, *The Hyphenated Family,* some of those preparations for Christmas. Referring to *Honigkuchen* he writes:

> Those golden-brown cookies were an essential part of the show. You couldn't imagine Christmas without them. Mother made them by the barrel and though she gave them away generously, we generally had some well into February.... I don't know what went into the composition of the "Honigkuchen," except that, paradoxically, honey was not among the ingredients and it was molasses which contributed the color. The dough was mixed and set aside for two weeks to ferment: *gaeren* was the word. It was another great day when mother finally rolled out the dough, dusted it with flour and stamped it with little tin forms into diamonds and circles and stars. We youngsters had a share in that, and in the further business of plastering an almond in the center of each cookie. We might help bake the cookies, but... that was the last we saw of them until Christmas.[1]

In this context, it might be mentioned that it was also the German-Americans who brought the Christmas tree and other traditions with them from the Old Country which help to make Christmas the family occasion it is today.

The "lager beer riots" in Chicago showed that the German equilibrium might be utterly disturbed if someone tried to interfere with the usual drinking customs. Dr. Levi D. Boone, elected mayor of Chicago in 1855, wanted to cure the Germans of their love for beer by raising the fee for liquor licenses by six hundred percent. He also wished to enforce the Sunday-closing ordinance, applying it only to places selling beer and not to establishments selling whiskey only. The Germans of Chicago (twenty-five percent of the population at the time) were in an uproar. The Irish joined them, because the mayor had also decreed that all policemen must be native Americans. On April 21, 1855, the combined forces of infuriated Germans and Irish threatened to storm City Hall, and rumors of civil insurrection went through the city. The mayor had second thoughts about the evil of drinking beer, and lifted the ban. The heavily German north side of the city quieted down, to become loud again with the more peaceful sounds of brass bands surrounded by people happily emptying and banging their steins on oaken tables.

The American beer brewing industry has traditionally been almost entirely in the hands of German-Americans, since the mid-nineteenth century. The lighter, more palatable beer brewed by the Forty-Eighters soon replaced the heavy English ale and whiskey. The founder of the Pabst Brewery was Jacob Best. When he first opened his brewery in 1844, the production of beer amounted only to three hundred barrels the first year. Later, under the management of Philipp Best, Emil Schandein, Friedrich and Gustav Pabst, the yearly production increased to two million barrels. Joseph Schlitz, who opened his brewery in 1849 in Milwaukee, had equal success. The four hundred barrels produced in 1849 were multiplied each year, and in 1907 increased to over 1.5 million barrels.

Numerous other breweries, large and small, were founded and are still managed by German-Americans throughout the United States. The number, however, is declining. Peter Hand, of the Peter Hand Brewery of Chicago, remarked in a recent newscast that of the eight hundred breweries existing in the United States a few decades ago, only two hundred escaped the economic squeeze. This probably does not mean that we are drinking less beer, but that hundreds of small breweries, like other small businesses, have fallen prey to our big business-oriented society.

Perhaps in contrast to popular belief, it should be noted that statistics tell us today that Belgians drink more beer, the French imbibe more wine, and the British down more whiskey per capita than do the Germans. It is nevertheless significant that, as John F. Kennedy stated in his *A Nation of Immigrants,*

> To the influence of the German immigrants in particular we owe the mellowing of the austere Puritan imprint on our daily lives. The Germans clung to their concept of the "Continental Sunday" as a day ... of relaxation, of picnics,

of visiting, of quiet drinking in beer gardens while listening to the music of a band.[2]

The mark of German-American influence upon our customs of food and drink may extend even farther than we have supposed, as noted by Wally Phillips in a column in the *Chicago Sun Times,* August 5, 1973:

... Anyway, tipplers are not about to abandon their favorite drink, that nip of nuclear numbness called the Martini. And if you have wondered about the origin of this potion, it was named after an Italian named Martini, right? Wrong. The martini is strictly German. It was invented by Johann Schwarzendorf (1741-1816), an organist and composer (he wrote, among other things, twelve operas) who, in some of his works, used the name Martini il Tedesco, which means "Martin the German." His concoction was brought to America by music lovers. Incidentally, Schwarzendorf's original martini was oliveless. The idea for the olive came from a French bartender employed in a New York hotel who figured the olive would conceal the raw alcohol taste. It didn't help much. The martini is still just a drink for thirsty souls who want a fast alcohol jolt, and Schwarzendorf's broth still has the fastest. But I'm glad Schwarzendorf used the name martini. Can you imagine, after the fifth blast, telling the barkeep: "Gimme another Schwarz&$!! ½ ⅝ ¾!"

15
Social and Labor Reform

The Industrial Revolution of the nineteenth century created a large labor force which was widely exploited by its employers. Most employers had adopted a superior standpoint. They expressed the same feelings toward their workers as they did toward their machines: "When they are old and of no further use, they are to be cast into the street." Labor was considered a commodity that would in the long run be governed solely and absolutely by the law of supply and demand.

Such views obviously needed reform. Among those whose voices called for protection of the rights of workers were many German-Americans, including Wilhelm Weitling. Born in Magdeburg, Germany, in 1808, Weitling came to America in 1846 at the invitation of a group of Free-Soilers to take charge of the publication of their journal. Shortly before his arrival, however, the journal, *Die Volkstribuene,* ceased publication, so Weitling turned his efforts to other concerns. He began to organize workmen's lodges to sponsor a program of state socialism:

Weitling's program was essentially to arm the proletariat, physically and intellectually, for the coming social revolution. He had plans for a labor bank to provide for an issue of paper money based on all capital goods. All inheritances and all church and unused property were to be confiscated by the State. All wealth created by work was to be stored in government magazines and used as a basis for currency to be issued by the government. The form of government somewhat approximated a workers' soviet. Workers, employers, and farmers were to turn their products over to the government in exchange for paper, thus eliminating—so Weitling thought—the capitalist profit system and the middleman. Guilds of workers and employers were to fix the value of all products and determine the amount of currency to be issued in exchange for them.[1]

This program appealed only to a fraction of German-Americans as the General Workmen's Convention proved in the fall of 1850, in Philadephia. Forty-four delegates (all from cities which had large German populations and representing forty-four hundred members) met to discuss the means of propaganda, education, and Weitling's proposals for the founding of a Labor Exchange Bank. The congress resolved to publish *Die Republik* in a monthly edition of four thousand eight hundred copies and adopted a new name: *Allgemeiner Arbeiterbund* (General Workingmen's League). The ultimate goal should be a World Republic:

The first step toward this World Republic was the purchase by the League of a thousand-acre farm in Iowa. Conditions for admission were easy: ten dollars, good health and good behaviour. "Communia" sheltered forty persons in 1852. All work was done in common and at the same time care was taken, that the different types of labor were rotated. Weitling's Workingmen's League enjoyed but a short life. His newspaper failed because it was never adapted to a laborer's intellect. Torn by quarrels, "Communia" ran into debts and was finally auctioned off in 1853. Weitling retired from public life, became a clerk in the Bureau of Immigration and devoted his last years to astronomy![2]

In spite of this failure, Weitling's followers advocated many reforms such as homestead legislation, protection against mortgage foreclosures, the single tax, public libraries, adult education, and a program of public works which were eventually to be realized, perhaps in part as a result of their early attempts at formulation of these ideas.

The Civil War and the slavery issue pushed the labor movement into the background. Many German-American labor leaders, among them Gustav Struve, Josef Weydemeyer, Fritz Annecke, August Willich, Rudolf Rosa, and Fritz Jacobi, went to war in 1861, and some won commissions in the Union army.

The end of the Civil War brought a revival of the labor movement:

The first Socialist party in America, which was founded in New York in 1867 and was very short-lived, developed from a German Communist club and the German Workers' Society of New York City. Most of the members of the Socialist Labor party of North America, founded in Newark in 1877, were Germans, and for the next fifteen years German was used in its conventions. Exiled German Socialists, driven out by Bismarck's persecution, were welcomed with open arms in the United States and added new strength to the movement. The *New Yorker Volkszeitung,* established in 1878 and edited by Dr. Adolph Douai, was the organ of the Socialist Labor party and was for years the leading Socialist paper in the United States. In 1889, there were at least eight important German Socialist dailies in the United States. The executive board of the First International in America consisted of three Germans, two Irish, two French, one Swede, and one Italian. In the 1870s and 1880s, many Germans became interested in the anarchist movement. August Spies, publisher of the Chicago *Arbeiterzeitung,* was one of those hanged in connection with the Haymarket riot, and the movement received a staggering blow from this unfortunate incident and the trial that followed. Of the ten indicted for murder, eight were Germans.[3]

The Haymarket riot in Chicago on May 4, 1886, was the

climax of wide-spread unemployment and labor unrest following the financial crisis of 1873. Although the anarchist leadership in Chicago was predominantly German at that time, the German community on the whole was rather conservative, opposing the anarchists and expressing satisfaction with the court's action. Seven years after the Haymarket riot, John Peter Altgeld lost the re-election for governor and any other political ambitions he had. Altgeld wrote an eighteen-thousand-word document justifying the pardon of Michael Schwab, Samuel Fielden, and Oscar Neebe. He was convinced that the men had been convicted for their radical views, because none of the accused could be connected with the throwing of the bomb by which one policeman was killed. The explosion of the bomb caused an indiscriminate firing, as a result of which seven policemen were killed and about sixty wounded, while on the laborers' side, four were killed and about fifty wounded.

The Haymarket riot had other after-effects: Though the trial of the anarchists was the "grossest travesty on justice ever perpetrated in an American court," still the anarchists had been most violent in their revolutionary agitation, and were felt to have been a menace to society. Such prompt and sweeping punishment cut away the very roots of anarchism in this country, and the good effect was also felt by the Socialist Labor party, who were rid of their dangerous internal enemy. The further history of the latter party showed a struggle between two factions, the one advocating alliance with labor unions and attempting to form an independent political party in spite of defeat at the polls, the other, conservative, arguing upon the futility of entering the political field, resenting Americanization, and counseling refusal to vote with any party until the time should be ripe for their socialistic theories. The former faction entered various alliances at different times until they formed a permanent union with the Social Democratic party of which the labor leader Eugene V. Debs and German socialist Victor L. Berger were the principal organizers. This party after the union was renamed the Socialist party, though in some states the name Social Democratic party remains in use. The other faction of the Socialist

Labor party remained conservative, and retained the name
Socialist Labor party.[4]

Except for Victor L. Berger, who was elected to Congress from the Fifth Wisconsin District, the Socialist party
was not represented in Congress. The party has been more
successful in local politics. In Milwaukee, for example,
Daniel Webster Hoan, half-Irish and half-German, was
elected to the mayor's office six times from 1916 to 1940.
When I arrived in Milwaukee in 1952, another member of
the Socialist party, Frank Zeidler, was mayor of the city.
He was praised by my former professor of German, William
Dehorn of Marquette University, as an A-student in his
German courses and as an excellent mayor who accom-
plished much for the common man.

Today, the leadership of most big labor unions is pri-
marily in the hands of Irish-Americans. The German-
Americans, however, continue to be well represented in the
labor movement in modern times by such men as the late
Walter Philip Reuther, president of the United Automobile
Workers, and many others.

Part 2

German-Americans
in
U.S. Military History

16
The Frontier Wars

Of the four wars between England and France on American soil, the last, from 1754 to 1763, was the most significant in terms of the involvement of German settlers. Both European powers tried to enlist the Indians as allies. The Huron, Ottawa, Miami, Illinois, and Shawnee fought on the French side, while England sought the help of the so-called Six Nations, consisting of the Iroquois, Mohawk, Oneida, Cayuga, Seneca, and Tuscarora. The fiercest fights occurred along the Ohio River—both sides claiming its territory. The French maintained that they had discovered it, while the English claimed to have settled it first.

In 1748, the Ohio Company, founded by the English government to further the fur trade and settlement of the region, engaged Christoph Gist (or Geist), a trapper of German descent, to explore and map the Ohio territory. Gist crossed the Allegheny Mountains and reached the Ohio in 1750. The Ottawa tribe respected him as the emissary of the English king, but received him coolly, since they were allies of the French. Gist, therefore, turned to the Wyandot settlements at the Muskingum River. To his surprise, he met a Pennsylvanian by the name of George Groghan who tried to get the permission of the Indians for a settlement by Pennsylvanian colonists. Both men went farther to the Delaware, Shawnee, and Miami Indians whom they persuaded to send representatives to a meeting with the Ohio Company at Logstown, a trading post in Ohio. The meeting took place in June 1752. Gist represented the Ohio Company, Colonel Frey the colony of Virginia. The Indians, however, fearing to lose their lands to either the French or the English, refused to give up titles of ownership.

In spite of this failure, the Ohio Company continued with its enterprise, sending surveyors and material over to start trading with the Indians as well to build a fort to protect their traders. The French, informed by their Indian allies of the undertaking, sent a force of a thousand men as well as a fleet of sixty ships and three hundred canoes to stop it on April 11, 1754. The Ohio Company yielded to this superior force, and the French immediately began the building of Fort Duquesne to protect their interests.

No blood had yet been shed. However, when a Virginia corps under the command of young George Washington fired at a French scouting troop, open war began. The English war plan, briefly sketched, was to form four military expeditions: the first under General Edward Braddock was to take Fort Duquesne, the second under General Shirley was to take Fort Niagara at Lake Ontario and march from there into Canada, the third under William Johnson intended to take Fort Crown Point at Lake Champlain, while the task of the fourth was to drive the French out of Nova Scotia. General Braddock started his campaign with two thousand men in the spring of 1755. On July 9, his army was ambushed and suffered a terrible defeat. Half of his troops and sixty-three officers were either wounded or killed. If it had not been for George Washington and his Virginian militia covering the retreat, the loss would have been complete.

Up to the time of this tragic defeat, the Indians living among the white settlers in the East had, in general, been peaceful mainly through the efforts of Conrad Weiser. Conrad had spent a year among the Mohawk learning their language and customs, as he tells us in his autobiography:

A chief of the Maqua (Mohawk) nation, named Quayant
visited my father, and they agreed that I should go with
Quayant into his country to learn the Mohawk language.
I accompanied him, and reached the Mohawk country in
the latter part of November, and lived with the Indians;
here I suffered much from the excessive cold, for I was
badly clothed, and towards spring also from hunger, for
the Indians had nothing to eat. I was frequently obliged
to hide from drunken Indians. Towards the end of July,
I returned to my father, and had learned the greater part
of the Mohawk language. There were always Mohawks
among us hunting, so that there was always something for
me to do in interpreting, but without pay.[1]

In 1732 Weiser became the official interpreter for Pennsylvania. The Indians trusted him, because he was "a good
and true man, and has spoken their words and our words—
not his own."[2] When the Indians of the Six Nations feuded
with the Cherokee and Catawba and were disturbing the
peace of the white settlers in their destructive wars against
each other, Weiser brought about a truce and then an alliance in 1737. In the summer of 1742, Weiser succeeded in
appeasing the Indians aroused by land robberies committed
against them. He even secured their help against a threatened French invasion.

In 1745 when the Six Nations were again about to over-
run the white settlements on the Mohawk in revenge for
land robberies, Governor Clinton of New York sent Weiser
to mediate. He not only pacified the Indians but also gained
their friendship. Before Gist had represented the Ohio Company in Logstown, Weiser had been sent there by the governor of Pennsylvania in 1748 with presents for the Indians
to persuade them from forming an alliance with the French.
He could, at the same time, observe the French settlements
and forts in the Ohio Valley, as well as the Indians allied
with them. This experience was invaluable when, in 1754,
he had to convince the Six Nations to remain in the English
camp against the French and their allies, the hostile Indians
of the Ohio Valley.

Conrad Weiser went twice with Moravian missionaries

to the Indians. He accompanied Count Zinzendorf to Wyoming on the Susquehanna to protect the count's life; and he went with Bishop Spangenberg to the Great Council Fire to beg land for the exiled Christian Indians from the Six Nations. Weiser spoke with authority when he advised the Moravian missionaries to:

> take up their abode in the midst of the Indians and strive to make themselves thorough masters of the language, conform as far as possible to their dress, manners, and customs, yet reprove their vices; translate the Bible in their own language ... study the Indian tunes and melodies, and convey to them the gospel in such melodies in order to make an abiding impression; and patiently wait for the fruits of their labors.[3]

He also did not hesitate to condemn the selling of liquor to the Indians: "If rightly considered, death without judge or jury to any man that carries rum to sell to any Indian town is the only remedy to prevent that trade, for nothing else will do. It is an abomination before God and man."[4]

After Braddock's defeat in 1755 all white settlers on the frontier were defenseless against French-Indian attacks; and Conrad Weiser, in spite of old age, took a prominent part in the defense. At the beginning of the hostilities, Governor Morris wrote him, "I heartily commend your courage and zeal, and that you may have greater authority, I have appointed you a colonel by the commission herewith. I leave it to your judgement and discretion, which I know are great, to do what is best for the safety of the people and the service of the Crown."[5] Weiser did not betray the governor's trust.

In 1756 he busied himself posting soldiers, attending councils, and sending troops to protect harvesters from Indian attacks. In July of 1757, Conrad attended a council at Easton. He was filled with hope because "the Indians are altogether good-humored, and Teedyuscing [the mighty chief of the Delaware] behaves very well, and I have not seen him quite drunk since I came to this town."[6] But in October of the same year he had to send a message to the governor, "It is certain that the enemy are numerous on the frontiers, and the people are coming away very fast.... It has now come so far that murder is committed almost every day ... so fly with my family I cannot do, I must stay if they all go."[7]

Weiser was able to collect fifty-six good, strong wagons for General Forbes' expedition against Fort Duquesne in 1758. When he learned that the governor had acted unfriendly to a delegation of his Indian friends, he wrote with vigor and frankness, "I will say that he does not act the part of a well-wisher to his majesty's people. You may let him know so. Here is my hand to my saying so. I am, sir, a loyal subject and a well-wisher to my country, Conrad Weiser."[8] In 1760, three years before the French and Indian wars were settled, Conrad Weiser died. His Indian comrades and friends visited his grave to mourn for many years after, and some confessed at one of the conferences at Easton, "We are at a great loss, we sit in darkness by the death of Conrad Weiser; since his death we cannot so well understand each other."[9]

The colonial authorities found an excellent replacement for Conrad Weiser in Christian Frederick Post, a Moravian missionary. Post spoke the Delaware language and knew the Indians well. He had lived among them and married a Christian Indian woman. His mission was to prevail upon the Indians to withdraw their alliance from the French. We learn from Post's journal how difficult and dangerous this task was. When an Indian guide told him that he had sold his life to the French, but was unfortunately prevented from keeping the contract to kill him, Post replied, "I am resolved to go forward, taking my life in my hands as one ready to part with it for your good."[10] After many long conferences and councils Post's peace offers were finally accepted, and the Delaware, Shawnee and Mingo were no longer enemies of the English. "In consequence thereof," Post wrote proudly, "the French were obliged to abandon the whole Ohio Country to General Forbes after destroying with their own hands their strong fort of Duquesne."[11] The French who had prevailed on the battlefield just a few weeks before by victory

over part of Forbes' army under Major Grant, had to desert
their stronghold as a result of the persuasive power of the
Moravian missionary in dealing with the Indians.

During the last decade of the French-Indian wars, white
settlers suffered immensely. The German settlements on the
frontier were no exception. In Pennsylvania the first blow
fell upon the Moravian mission station at Gnadenhuetton on
the Mahanoy. The Indians shot several of the missionary
families and then set fire to their houses. In two weeks the
entire border was deserted, and terrified people crowded
into the hastily fortified settlements of the United Brethren
at Nazareth and Bethlehem. From Bethlehem the brethren
sent a plea to the governor:

> Your Honor can easily guess at the trouble and conster-
> nation we must be in on this occasion in these parts. As to
> Bethlehem, we have taken all the precautions in our power
> for our Defence; we have taken all our little Infants from
> Bethlehem for the greater security. Although our gracious
> King and parliament have been pleased to exempt those
> among us of tender conscience from bearing arms, yet there
> are many amongst us who make no scruple of defending
> themselves against such cruel savages. But, alas, what can
> we do, having very few arms and little or no ammunition,
> and we are now, as it were, become the frontiers.[12]

There is no doubt that the German frontiersmen did
their share in fighting the Indians. Even the otherwise pacifist German sectarians took part as we learn from a report
by Conrad Weiser: "I believe, that people in general up here
will fight. I had two or three long beards in my company,
one a Mennonite, who declared he would live and die with
his neighbors. He had a good gun with him."[13] The Quaker
government of Pennsylvania province, because of its spirit
of nonresistance, was slow to take measures for the defense
of its frontier. It was finally forced into action by a band of
frontiersmen, among them four hundred Germans, who
brought to Philadelphia a wagon filled with the mutilated
bodies of friends and relatives slain by the Indians on the
frontier. One of the measures taken was the formation of

the "Royal American" regiment raised among the German and Swiss settlers of Maryland and Pennsylvania. As they were all zealous Protestants, and in general, strong, hardy men accustomed to the climate, it was judged that a regiment of good and faithful soldiers might be raised out of them, particularly proper to oppose the French. But to this end it was necessary to appoint some officers who understood military discipline, and could speak the German language.

The English government employed some Swiss officers who had been in the service of the Dutch republic, among them Henry Bouquet, a native of Bern, Switzerland, who became lieutenant colonel of the new organization. Bouquet arrived in Philadelphia in 1756. He and his Royal Americans took part in taking Fort Duquesne under General Forbes. After Forbes's return to Philadelphia and subsequent death, Henry Bouquet succeeded to the command of Fort Pitt, as Fort Duquesne was now called in honor of the English prime minister of the time. The Royal Americans saw action on many fronts. Some battalions of the regiment participated in the campaign against French Arcadia; others were part of the expedition against Crown Point. They helped to take Louisburg from the French in 1758, and they were among the conquerors of Fort Niagara the following year. Their proudest moment came at the fall of Quebec, when the regiment won the right to its motto, *Celer et Audax*, "Swift and Bold." Royal Americans manned the first English garrisons of Canada, when that province finally surrendered to England in 1760. They also were part of the garrison of Morro Castle which the English built during their occupation of Cuba in 1762. Many of them did garrison duty in the long chain of scattered forts or blockhouses extending from Philadelphia to Fort Pitt, Sandusky, and Detroit. When Pontiac's war broke out in 1763, most of those "military hermits" were surprised by the Indians and either killed or captured. Fort Pitt, which was defended gallantly by the Royal Americans, was the only one of the western posts to remain besides the besieged Detroit and Niagara.

To break the Indian siege of Fort Pitt, Henry Bouquet left Philadelphia with five hundred Royal Americans, who had just returned from Havana. At Bushy Run, twenty-five miles from the fort, they made contact with the enemy. The Indians believed they could easily ambush and destroy Bouquet and his Royals; but Bouquet defeated the Indians, ended the siege of Fort Pitt, as well as Pontiac's war, and rendered the frontiers safe. The colonial authorities commissioned Bouquet to start peace talks with the Indians and to demand the return of prisoners held by the Indians. On November 12, 1764, peace was made with the Delaware, Seneca, and Shawnee, who returned two hundred and six white prisoners. A. B. Faust summarized the accomplishments of the troops under Bouquet:

> In the defense of the frontier during the French and Indian War, the Royal Americans made a glorious record. This regiment consisted of four battalions of one thousand men each. Fifty of the officers were to be foreign Protestants, while the enlisted men were to be raised principally from the German settlers in America. The immediate commander was Colonel (later General) Bouquet, a Swiss by birth, an English officer by adoption, and a Pennsylvanian by naturalization, the last a distinction conferred upon him for his campaign in Western Pennsylvania, where he with Forbes wiped out the disgrace of Braddock's defeat. The rank and file of the regiment were German and Swiss settlers of Pennsylvania, young men enlisted for three years, and they saw service in all parts of the colonies. A list of their campaigns is as follows:
> 1757. First Battalion in Indian wars.
>   Five companies under Stanwix in Pennsylvania.
>   Third Battalion at Fort Hunter and Fort William Henry.
>   Second and Fourth at Louisbourg.
>   First Battalion under Bouquet in South Carolina.
>   First and Fourth at Crown Point and Ticonderoga.
> 1758. Second and Third Battalions at Louisbourg.
>   First and Fourth under Bouquet and Forbes at Fort Duquesne.
> 1759. Fourth Battalian under Prideaux at Fort Niagara.
>   Second and Third under Wolfe at Quebec.
>   Fourth under Haldiman at Oswego.

First under Amherst at Lake Champlain.

Fourth under Sir William Johnson, Bouquet, Stanwix, and Wolfe at Quebec.

1760. First, Second, and Third at Quebec.

1761. First in Virginia.

1762. Third at Martinique and Havana.

1763. First under Bouquet at Bushy Run and Pittsburgh.

These campaigns made veterans of the Pennsylvania
boys and prepared a nucleus of self-reliant soldiers for the
coming war of the Revolution.[14]

17

The German-Americans during the War of Independence

When England tried to force her American colonies to share her worldwide obligations and costly responsibilities by imposing ever increasing tax burdens, a severe conflict was unavoidable. Again and again the American colonists had tried to alleviate the unbearable taxes and to compromise, but the English Crown, George III, remained stubborn and unyielding. In consequence, difficulties arose between the colonial authorities and the colonists, leading to many incidents of a more or less violent nature. On April 19, 1775, shots were exchanged at Lexington between the militia of Massachusetts and British soldiers, marking the point of no return: the military struggle for American independence had begun.

It was not surprising that most German-Americans were on the side of the Revolutionary forces. They had left Germany to escape from the hands of unjust, bigoted rulers and were now only too eager to keep their hard-won freedom for themselves and their children. It is true that many German sectarians as well as English Quakers did not favor the Revolution because of their spirit of nonresistance and their pacifist beliefs. In the progress of the struggle for freedom, however, they made up for their refusal to bear arms by furnishing much needed supplies and paying much higher taxes. The Moravians of North Carolina, for instance, cheerfully paid three times the amount of tax levied upon them. Moreover, the large community houses of the United Brethren at Reading, Lancaster, Bethlehem, and elsewhere served as hospitals, and the brothers and sisters tended to the needs of the sick and wounded soldiers of the Revolutionary army.

The German Lutheran and Reformed churches of Philadelphia vigorously supported the cause of armed resistance against the oppression and despotism of the English government. Both these church groups in 1775 sent a forty-page pamphlet to the Germans of New York and North Carolina urging them to form—as they themselves had done—militia companies and corps of sharpshooters. Muehlenberg and Schlatter, the patriarchs of the two denominations respectively, placed their whole authority behind the cause for freedom. Michael Schlatter, the leader of the Reformed church, served in spite of advanced age as a chaplain in the Revolutionary army as he had done previously in the French and Indian War.

Heinrich Muehlenberg's moral support was complemented by the active service of his son Peter, who had studied theology in Halle, Germany. Returning to the colonies in 1772, Peter hâd become the pastor of the Lutheran church at Woodstock, Virginia. Upon the recommendation of Patrick Henry, Peter Muehlenberg was made commander of the Eighth Virginia Regiment. In January 1776, he delivered his last sermon in the little church of Woodstock, ending it by claiming, "There is a time for preaching and praying, but also a time for battle, and that time has now arrived." He then took off his clerical robe and descended from the pulpit in the uniform of a Continental colonel. To the roll of drums, he marched to the open door. The people inside and outside the church cheered, and more than three hundred young men immediately joined Muehlenberg's regiment, to be followed by a hundred more the next day.

Muehlenberg proved to be a brave soldier, known to

friend and foe alike as "Devil's Pete," a curious name for a
cleric. On February 21, 1777, he was raised to the rank of
brigadier-general and put in charge of the First, Fifth, Ninth,
and Thirteenth Virginia Regiments. His men took part in
many encounters with the British at Charleston, Brandywine, Germantown, Monmouth, Stony Point, and Yorktown.
Following his distinguished military career, Peter Muhlenberg became active and prominent in political affairs. He
represented Pennsylvania three times in the United States
Congress, 1789-1791, 1793-1795, and 1799-1801. Later, he became superintendent of internal revenue and collector of
the port of Philadelphia.

According to a story recounted in Rufus W. Griswold's,
*The Republican Court: American Society in the Days of
Washington,* Peter Muehlenberg is responsible for the fact
that Washington and all succeeding presidents had to be con-
tent with the title, "Mr. President." While Chief Justice
John Jay of the United States Supreme Court proposed
shortly before the opening of Congress in 1789 that Washington should be addressed as "His Serene Highness, the President of the United States," Washington himself thought it
appropriate to be called "High Mightiness." At a dinner
Washington seriously asked his old hunting companion,
"Well, General Muehlenberg, what do you think of the title
of High Mightiness?" Muhlenberg laughed, and with his
reply set such lofty ideas to rest, "Why, General, if we were
certain that the office would always be held by men as large
as yourself or my friend Wynkoop, it would be appropriate
enough, but if by chance a president as small as my opposite
neighbor should be elected, it would become ridiculous."[1]

The sermons of Peter Muehlenberg had early aroused
the Germans of Virginia to the cause of freedom and independence. The first company from the South to join Washington's troops at Cambridge was under the command of
Captain Daniel Morgan and consisted largely of German
frontiersmen of Frederick County, Virginia. On June 17,
1775, they met at Morgan's Spring near Shepherdstown,
where they agreed to meet again fifty years later. On that
appointed day in 1825, there were but four of the Virginia

riflemen alive: the two Dedinger brothers, Henry of Virginia and George Michael of Kentucky; Lauck of Winchester and Hulse of Wheeling—names which attested to the German makeup of Morgan's corps. They left for battle in 1775 armed with tomahawks and rifles and dressed in hunting shirts and moccasins; they travelled lightly and covered the six hundred miles to Boston in fifty-four days.

When they approached the camp of Cambridge, they were spotted by Washington, who jumped from his horse and with tears in his eyes, shook hands with each man of the Virginia company. These sharpshooters served valiantly and efficiently during the siege of Boston, aiming their rifles especially at the British officers, who were killed or wounded in such numbers as to cause great concern in the English Parliament. The Winchester rifles which had been perfected by German gunsmiths no doubt helped to win the war. Morgan and one hundred of his men were later captured by the British in the attempt to take Quebec.

The battle of Long Island almost turned out to be disastrous for Washington's army. Among Lord Stirling's brigade covering Washington's retreat were many Germans from Maryland and Pennsylvania. According to a contemporary estimate, it was the First Pennsylvania Battalion that suffered the heaviest loss: "Lord Stirling's brigade sustained the hottest of the enemy's fire; they were all surrounded by the enemy and had to fight their way through the blaze of their fire. They fought and fell like Romans."[2] In another historical report the battle is called "the Thermopylae of the War of Independence, and the Pennsylvania Germans are . . . its Spartans."

To boost the morale of his troops in retreat, Washington needed a victory. He obtained it at Trenton, crossing the Delaware on Christmas Night, 1776, in a surprise attack on Britain's Hessian mercenaries commanded by Colonel Rall. Among Washington's troops were many German soldiers such as those of the Maryland militia under the command of Colonel Nicholas Hausegger. A cousin of the Hessian commander, with the same name and the same rank, belonged to the Maryland militia. The American Colonel Rall was a

cobbler in civilian life and had come from the Palatinate to
the colonies several years earlier. It was his troop that found
the Hessian colonel—in bed. The latter put up a good fight,
but, heavily wounded, he was forced to surrender to his
cousin, the American colonel.

The action at Trenton had been no more than a raid.
Casualties on both sides had been low—about thirty British
and five Americans. But Washington captured about nine
hundred men and officers, whom he marched through the
streets of Philadelphia to raise the spirits of its citizens.
Despite Washington's subsequent victory at Princeton and
his efforts at training and regrouping during the early
months of 1777, his army was only about four thousand men
strong. The British remained set upon their original plan of
cutting off the New England states from the rest of the
colonies.

To accomplish this goal, General Burgoyne began his
march down from Canada in the middle of June 1777. A
British expedition, which was moving up the Hudson from
New York, planned to aid him. In addition, Colonel St. Leger
was to come from the west to join Burgoyne at Albany. St.
Leger's job was to subdue American resistance in the Mohawk Valley and make its fertile fields the granary of Burgoyne's army. The plan was foiled by the heroic fight of
General Herkimer and his four battalions which consisted
largely of German settlers. Herkimer and his men had gained
military experience during the French and Indian War.

When the first storms of the Revolutionary War swept
through the Mohawk and Schoharie valleys, the settlers had
to get organized because they could not wait for help from
the New York State government. Thus, in the summer of
1775, the Committee of Safety in Tyron County formed four
battalions of militia in preparation for the coming encounter
with the combined forces of the British, Indians, and former
neighbors who had turned Royalists. Foremost among the
latter group was Sir William Johnson of Tyron County. He
had been successful in keeping the Indians loyal during the
French and Indian War and when he became a Tory, he
carried the Indians with him. Herkimer tried in vain to per-

suade the Iroquois Chief Thayendanegea, known both for his might and intelligence, to side with the colonists. The English had convinced many of the Indians that their king across the ocean was the stronger master. Moreover, the Indians themselves were looking forward to the plunder of rich farms and fat herds in the Mohawk and Schoharie valleys. On July 17, 1777, friendly Oneida Indians informed Herkimer that St. Leger was on his way with seven hundred soldiers and a thousand Indians under the leadership of Thayendenegea, and Herkimer called his people to arms with the proclamation:

> Whereas it appears certain that the enemy, about two thousand strong, Christians and savages are arrived at Oswego with the intention to invade our frontiers...as soon as the enemy approaches every male person, being in health, from sixteen to sixty years of age, in this county shall...march to oppose the enemy with vigor as true patriots for the defence of their country. And those above sixty years of age shall assemble armed at the places where women and children will be gathered together, not doubting that the Almighty power upon our humble prayers and sincere trust in Him will then graciously succor our arms in battle, for our just cause.[3]

In order to gain access to the Mohawk Valley, St. Leger had to take Fort Stanwix, which was defended by a small force under Colonel Gansevoort. Herkimer sent runner Adam Helmer to the fort to arrange for a simultaneous attack on the British forces, to begin at the firing of three signal guns. But Herkimer's own men were impatient, and urged their leader to attack immediately, without waiting. Herkimer tried to calm his troops. "I am placed over you as a father and guardian," he told them, "and I will not lead you into difficulties from which I may not be able to extricate you."[4] When the other officers denounced him as a coward who was secretly in league with the Tories, Herkimer told them, "If you will have it so, the blood will be upon your heads."[5]

Meanwhile, St. Leger had learned of the approach of

the Palatines and had prepared an ambush. On August 6, 1777, as Herkimer was leading his troops along a supply road toward the fort, St. Leger's Indians attacked where the road dipped down into a dark, wooded ravine. The rear guard (under the command of Colonel Fischer, who had been the loudest accuser of Herkimer) turned and fled, and most of the men were killed in the process. The rest of the troops, however, formed a circle and defended themselves success- fully. As he was riding along inspecting the line of defense, Herkimer was wounded by a musket ball which smashed his left knee. He refused to leave the battle and ordered his men to place him, on his saddle, under a beech tree, where he could direct the fierce fighting. He soon noticed that the Indians waited until a gun was discharged and then rushed forward to tomahawk the soldier while he reloaded his gun. Herkimer immediately changed tactics; he had two men placed behind a bush or tree, one firing and one loading, thereby covering each other and causing heavy casualties among the Indians.

The Indians were soon reinforced by a Tory regiment, Johnson's Greens, but the Germans did not despair, and only became fiercer in their fight against their former neigh- bors, whom they considered traitors. A savage hand-to-hand battle developed, but was interrupted by a thunderstorm. When finally the signal of three gun shots was heard from Fort Stanwix, the decimated Indians took to their heels, forcing their allies to flee the battlefield with them. The battle of Oriskany thoroughly discouraged and demoralized the Indians, making them unreliable allies for the British. When news reached the British camp that General Arnold was coming to aid the besieged fort, St. Leger, already weak- ened by the loss of his Indian allies, hastily lifted the siege on August 22, 1777, abandoned his tents and ammunition, and retreated.

Although the brave Palatines had lost one-fourth of their forces, which had been eight hundred strong, they had foiled the British plan of cutting off the New England colonies from the Southern colonies, and this contributed indirectly to Burgoyne's surrender at Saratoga. In George Washington's judgment, "It was Herkimer who first reversed the gloomy scene ... [who] served from love of country, not for reward. He did not want a Continental command or money."

Herkimer died nine days after the battle of Oriskany. His leg had had to be amputated. When a hemorrhage occurred, Herkimer said, "I am going to follow my leg." With the words of the Thirty-Eight Psalm on his lips, "O Lord, rebuke me not in Thy wrath," the defender of the Mohawk Valley passed away. By October of 1777, Congress had approved five hundred dollars to erect a monument in honor of the hero of the battle of Oriskany. The state of New York kept the memory of Herkimer alive, giving his name to the town of his birth and the county in which he lived.

The victory by the Continental army under General Gates at Saratoga prevented the British from driving a wedge between the Northern and Southern colonies. Moreover, Saratoga proved that the Revolutionary army could defeat a British army, and won over England's enemies, France and Spain, to the cause of American independence. Washington's army, defeated by the British at Brandywine Creek and Germantown and spending the winter of 1777-1778 at Valley Forge, needed all the help it could get. Aid came from Germany in the person of Baron von Steuben, who had served honorably under Frederick the Great of Prussia. Arriving from Paris with a letter of recommendation by Benjamin Franklin, Steuben was accepted by Congress and sent directly to Washington at Valley Forge. He arrived in February 1778, and Washington received him immediately at his headquarters. In a previous letter Steuben had made a favorable impression on Washington, saying,

> The object of my greatest ambition is to render your country all the services in my power and to deserve the title of a citizen of America by fighting for the cause of liberty. If the distinguished ranks in which I have served in Europe should be an obstacle, I had rather serve under your excellency as a volunteer than to be subject of discontent to such deserving officers as have already distinguished themselves amongst you.[6]

As soon as consideration for the feelings of the officers allowed it, Steuben was made inspector general of the Continental army. Part of this job was to retrain the Revolutionary army so that it could fight more effectively against the disciplined Redcoats. From the very beginning Steuben proceeded with tact and good judgment of the situation. He wrote to a friend in Germany, "In the first place, the genius of this nation is not in the least to be compared with that of the Prussians, Austrians, or French. You say to your soldier, 'Do this,' and he does it, but I am obliged to say, 'This is the reason why you ought to do that,' and then he does it."[7]

Some of the soldiers were rather naive, and not able to tell left from right. Steuben, therefore, had straw fastened to the right boot of the soldier and hay to the left; and then cadence could be called as, "*Hay*-foot, *straw* foot, a *belly* full of *bean* soup!" Most of the soldiers regarded the bayonet as a tool to barbecue meat on, rather than as a weapon. Steuben instructed them in the use of the bayonet and the training paid off the following year when the American forces took the fortress of Stony Point at bayonet point—without a shot being fired.

To hasten the task of retraining an army, Steuben selected one company which he drilled personally and from which he then chose drill sergeants to train other companies. He also chose a group of young officers whom he called his "*sansculottes*" who helped to supervise the training activities. One of those young captains, Benjamin Walker, wrote that the baron often lost his temper when the soldiers failed to execute the proper maneuver and

> began to swear in German, then in French, and then in both languages together. When he had exhausted his artillery of foreign oaths, he would call to his aides, "My dear Walker and my dear Duponceau, come and swear for me in English. These fellows won't do what I bid them." A good-natured smile went through the ranks and at last the maneuver or the movement was properly performed.[8]

After only a few months, Steuben reaped the fruit of his labor, and in May 1788 the alliance of France with the United States was celebrated with a big maneuver. The maneuver was a complete success, and at the following banquet, General Washington expressed his gratitude and gave Steuben a letter from Congress containing the promotion to major general. The officers on Washington's staff wished to retain their previous military system and Steuben had to convince them that his new system was the better one. This was not an easy task, as the Baron commented in a letter to a friend:

> My good republicans wanted everything in the English style; our great and good allies wanted everything in the French mode, and when I presented a plate of sauerkraut dressed in the Prussian style, they all wanted to throw it out the window. Nevertheless, by the force of proving by Goddams that my cookery was the best, I overcame the prejudices of the former; but the second liked me as little in the forests of America as they did on the plains of Rossbach (a Franco-Prussian battlefield on which Steuben had served under Frederick the Great). Do not, therefore, be astonished if I am not painted in very bright colors in Parisian circles.[9]

Steuben spiced his "plate of sauerkraut" with American touches by forming groups of light infantry which fought from behind trees and bushes Indian-style. Combining old and new techniques, Steuben showed his intelligence. He wrote down his regulations in French; his aide Duponceau then translated them into English. These came to be known as *Steuben's Regulations* or, *The Blue Book*. This handbook served for a long time as a guide to officers in the performance of their military duties. *The Blue Book* also established a definite order in the requisition and management of supplies, because a reform in drill was but a small part of the job of the inspector general. To make sure that his regulations were followed, Steuben undertook tours of inspection from time to time. Steuben's adjutant, William North, was present when the inspector general and his assistants inspected a brigade for a full seven hours, and he recorded:

> Every man not present was to be accounted for; if in camp, sick or well, he was produced or visited; every musket was handled and searched, cartridge boxes were opened; even the flints and cartridges counted; knapsacks

were unslung and every article of clothing was spread on
the soldier's blanket and tested by his little book.[10]

His system of reviews, reports, and inspection gave efficiency to the soldier, confidence to the commander, and
saved the treasury not less than $600,000.[11]

In the winter of 1780-1781 Steuben again performed the
job of "the drill-master of the army." Out of the Virginia
militia he created a well-disciplined army for General
Greene, who had been appointed commander of the southern
army. Greene's army not only checked the invasion which
resulted from the acts of the traitor Benedict Arnold, but
also fought with distinction at Yorktown, the decisive last
battle of the War of Independence. Steuben's service was
especially welcome at Yorktown, because he was the only
American officer present who had taken part in a siege.
On October 17, 1781, British General Cornwallis surrendered.
The division which Steuben commanded happened to be in
the trenches closest to the enemy that day. Steuben, therefore, had the privilege of being in command when the
enemy's flag was lowered. Lafayette tried to replace Steuben
in overseeing the conditions of surrender, but Washington
allowed Steuben to remain in command. So it was that Steuben accepted the British request for surrender, an honor
highly prized by all the superior officers. On October 19,
Steuben's forces were among the first to enter Yorktown,
proudly displaying the flag of the victorious United States.

After the war Steuben continued to serve his adopted
country. He helped in planning West Point Military Academy.
To ensure that all future officers were broadly educated men,
Steuben insisted on full professorships in history, geography,
civil and international law, eloquence and belles-lettres. He
also proposed a plan of fortifications for New York. Steuben
was chosen a regent of the University of New York and
was the president of the German Society of New York from
1785 to 1794. He died in 1794 and was buried at his estate
in Oneida County, New York. To this day the Steuben Society keeps the memory of this veteran of the War of Independence alive, honoring him every year with parades,
notably in New York and Chicago.

Another hero of the Revolutionary War was John de Kalb, a baron by his own efforts. He was born Hans Kalb in 1721 in Germany, the son of a Franconian peasant. Though not a nobleman by birth, he became one in deed and character. He left home at the age of sixteen to join the army of France. In 1743 we find his name in a French army register as Lieutenant Jean de Kalb. Four years later he became a captain. Slowly but steadily he climbed the ladder of military ranks, becoming next a major and in 1763, a colonel. He married the daughter of a Dutch millionaire and, as Baron de Kalb, assured for himself a position of influence and comfort in Europe. But the soldier in him made him join Lafayette in 1777 to offer his services in the cause of American independence. After his arrival in America he wrote to Congress, "General Washington has perhaps friends or deserving officers to whom he would give the preference. In such case I should be sorry my coming did in the least cross him or prevent his dispositions in this and in other respects. I will gladly and entirely submit to his commands and be employed as he shall think most convenient for the good of the service."[12] His offer was accepted and he served as a major general under Washington in New Jersey and Maryland with those states' strong contingent of German soldiers. He fought valiantly at the head of his troops in the ill-fated battle of Camden, where General Gates foolishly pitted his nearly untrained troops, who were exhausted by a long march in August heat, against the veteran regiments of Cornwallis. The historian Bancroft reports that the Virginia militia "ran like a torrent, and the general ran with them and faster, for he outdistanced the most terrified of the militia and was altogether ignorant of the fate of his army."[13] (This was certainly a very bad report of the hero of Saratoga, yet it was unfortunately true that by evening Gates was safely miles away from the site of the battle.) Kalb, however, held fast regardless of the odds as Bancroft recorded:

The division which Kalb commanded continued long in action, and never did troops show greater courage than those men of Maryland and Delaware. The horse of Kalb had been killed under him and he had been badly wounded; yet he continued to fight on foot. At last, in the hope of victory, he led a charge, drove the division under Rawdon, took fifty prisoners, and would not believe that he was not to gain the day, when Cornwallis poured against him a party of dragoons and infantry. Even then he did not yield until disabled by many wounds. The victory cost the British about five hundred of their best troops; "their great loss," wrote Marion, "is equal to a defeat." Except one hundred Continental Soldiers whom Gist conducted across the swamps through which the cavalry could not follow, every American corps was dispersed. Kalb lingered for three days. Opulent and happy in his wife and children, he gave to the United States his life and his example. Congress decreed him a monument.[14]

Besides other German officers, too many to mention, there were plain German militiamen who fervently pursued the course to freedom. A British traveller named Smyth experienced the heat of this fervor, when he was invited in 1775 to appear before the revolutionary committee of Frederickstown, Maryland. Smyth preferred to leave town, and the German patriots caught up with him, confronting him with the full force of the *"furor teutonicus."* He recorded his ordeal in his book, *A Tour in the United States of America,* and even attempted to imitate the speech of his captors by phonetic spelling:

> One said, "Got tamn you, how darsht you make an exshkape from this honorable committish?" "Fer flucht der dyvel," cried another, "how can you shtand so shtyff for King Shorsh akainst dish Koonterey?" "Sacramenter," roars out another, "dish committish will make Shorsh know how to behave himself"; and the butcher exclaimed, "I would kill all de English tieves as soon as Ich would kill van ox or van cow."[15]

After this experience Mr. Smyth was probably only too glad to get out of the country unharmed and return to England to record his story.

Another aggressive advocate of the Revolution was Christopher Ludwig. After an eventful life as a soldier and sailor in the European wars he settled down in Philadelphia in 1754. Following a trade he had learned in his native city of Giessen, Germany, he opened up a bakery in a section of Philadelphia called Laetitia Court. He was a prominent figure in his day. Tall and erect in stature, his commanding presence earned him the nickname "Governor of Laetitia Court." In 1776, at the age of fifty-five, he volunteered to become a member of the militia. In the same year he ran an advertisement in the *Staatsbote* for a man who knew how to make gunpowder.

When Governor Mifflin made a motion to raise money for the purchase of arms and ammunition, Christopher Ludwig saved the motion from being defeated by declaring in a loud voice with a heavy German accent, "Mr. President, I am of course only a poor gingerbread baker, but write me down for two hundred pounds."[16] In 1777, Congress appointed Ludwig superintendent of bakers and director of baking for the entire army; he was to furnish one hundred pounds of bread for every one hundred pounds of flour. "No," said he, "Christopher Ludwig does not wish to become rich by the war. He has enough. Out of hundred pounds of flour comes one hundred and thirty five pounds of bread, and so many will I give."[17] Because of this Washington called him his "honest friend."

Washington is said to have drunk many a toast to the health of his honest friend with the couplet, "Health and long life, to Christopher Ludwig and his wife." When the British took Philadelphia, they confiscated Ludwig's property, making him a poor man on his return. In 1797 during a yellow fever epidemic the old man himself worked at the bake oven to provide bread for the poor in that period of dire distress. Shortly before his death in 1809, someone wanted to sell him a biography of Washington, who had preceded him in death. "No," said the general's honest friend, "I am travelling fast to meet him. I shall hear all about it from his own mouth." He left his money to various chari-

table institutions and causes—most of it for the free education of poor children. The free school founded with his money
in 1872 was named in his honor, Ludwig's Institute.

Maria Ludwig was the maiden name of "Moll Pitcher,"
the heroine of Monmouth, but she was no relation to the
"honest baker." When her husband, a gunner in an artillery
company, was wounded, she joined him and nursed him back
to health. For seven years she accompanied him from battlefield to battlefield, attending to the sick and wounded soldiers
and carrying water to the fighting men in the heat of battle.
The soldiers were reported to have said, "Here comes Moll
with her pitcher," which accounts for her famous nickname.
She even helped her husband with his duties as a gunner,
and according to Private Joseph Plumb Martin of the Eighth
Connecticut, did it with courage and some style:

> While in the act of reaching for a cartridge and having
> one of her feet as far before the other as she could step, a
> cannon shot from the enemy passed directly between her
> legs without doing any other damage than carrying away
> all the lower part of her petticoat. Looking at it with ap-
> parent unconcern, she observed that it was lucky it did
> not pass any higher, for in that case it might have carried
> away something else, and continued her occupation. . . .[18]

At the battle of Monmouth Maria took over the job of
gunner when her husband fell wounded. By her bravery she
steadied the other soldiers who were in doubt whether to
fight or to retreat. Thus, the company stood its ground until
reinforcements arrived. Washington supposedly witnessed
the action and praised the woman. After the war Congress
gave her the rank of brevet captain and an annual pension
of forty dollars. A granddaughter of "Moll Pitcher" described her as a short, heavy-set woman with blue eyes and
reddish hair. Her grandchildren feared her for her rough,
brusque manners; and she is said to have been able to swear
like a trooper. Mrs. Alexander Hamilton remembers her as
"a little freckle-faced Irish lass," which seems to be correct,
except for Moll's nationality.

The Moravian Brothers and Sisters cared for the suffering Revolutionary soldiers on a larger scale than "Moll with her pitcher." The large community houses of the United Brethren were well suited as army hospitals. In Pennsylvania the German community centers at Bethlehem, Lititz, Ephrata, Easton, Allentown, Reading, and Lancaster became refuges for the sick and wounded. In North Carolina, the Moravian settlement of Bethabara also provided a hospital. The soldiers suffered not only from wounds but also from typhus, or "camp fever," as it was called. Bishop Ettwein, while caring for the sick at Bethlehem, lost a little son from fever brought home from the soldiers' bedsides. When the hospital at Lititz was filled with typhus patients, two doctors and five Brothers died of the sickness they had contracted by caring for the soldiers. For the dead soldiers, the Moravian brethren provided coffins and burial grounds. The mortality was high—so fearfully high that the number of deaths was kept secret. In addition to caring for the sick and wounded and burying the dead, the United Brethren helped the fighting men. In the bitter winter of 1777-1778 they supplied Washington's army at Valley Forge with much needed food and clothing. In many ways the German sectarians repaid the privilege granted to them by Congress in 1775 of not having to bear arms.

In the Carolinas and in Georgia, the United Brethren were not the only ones among the German settlers who supported the Revolution. In these colonies the Tories often outnumbered the Revolutionaries, and many Germans suffered because of their patriotism. The Tories and British troops of Cornwallis paid "rather expensive visits" to the church settlements of the Moravian Brothers, who were hard pressed to keep to their nonresistant principles. But other Germans were free to resist, and did. Michael Kalteisen, a prosperous merchant in Charleston, organized a German military company which later became known as the Ancient and Honorable German Fusiliers, which served with distinction throughout the Revolutionary War. To be sure, not all Germans were patriots, but German Tories remained the exception.

In Georgia most of the Salzburgers of Ebeneezer supported the cause of freedom. Among the provincials who met in Savannah in 1775 to adopt measures for protection against abuses by the English, the Salzburgers John Stirk, John Adam Treutlen, Jacob Wildhauer, John Florl, and Christopher Cramer represented their home districts. Most prominent among the Salzburgers mentioned was John Adam Treulten. He was well educated and the leader of the German congregation. Under the new Constitution Treutlen was elected the first governor of Georgia in May 1777. When the British burned down his home in 1778, he fled and joined the army of General Wayne. Truetlen was fifty-three years of age at that time, and he served as a quartermaster general throughout the war.

General Washington showed his faith in the loyalty of the German-Americans. When he suspected his first "bodyguard" or headquarters company of being infiltrated by Tories, he replaced them with German soldiers from Berks and Lancaster counties, Pennsylvania. This unit consisted of fourteen officers and fifty-three men, commanded by Major von Heer, who had served under Frederick the Great. They were with Washington from 1778 to the end of the war in 1783. Twelve of them served longer than any other American soldiers of the Revolutionary War; they had the honor of escorting the commander in chief to his home at Mount Vernon. The records show that all twelve received gifts and were discharged on December 10, 1783. Colonel John Johnson, a personal friend of Washington, stated that von Heer's troop consisted exclusively of Germans and that not a single officer or soldier understood a word of English.

If it is true that an army marches on its stomach, then three of the most important posts of the Continental army were held by Germans: Steuben, inspector general; Ludwig, superintendent of bakers; and Lutterloh, quartermaster general. Lutterloh first became a colonel on Washington's staff in 1777, and as Washington regarded him highly, he was made quartermaster general three years later.

One of the most difficult and responsible positions of the young emerging nation was held by a successful German merchant, Michael Hillegas, treasurer of Congress from 1775 to 1789. Hillegas published many national documents of great historical importance, including the Declaration of Independence and the Articles of Confederation.

David Rittenhouse, a Mennonite and an industrious scientist, left the peaceful banks of the Wissahickon to offer his knowledge to the cause of freedom. He was placed in charge of making arrangements for casting cannon, selection of a site for a Continental powder mill, conducting experiments for rifling cannon and musket balls, supervision of manufacture of saltpeter, and location of a magazine for military stores. He later became the first director of the U.S. Mint. A Tory poet scorned this political activity of a man of science, commenting, "A paltry statesman Rittenhouse became." There was nothing paltry, however, about the activity of this Mennonite, who helped the Revolutionaries without compromising his pacifist beliefs.

The German merchant Arnold Henry Dohrmann, stationed at Lisbon, Portugal, supported the American Revolution in an extraordinary way. By selling weapons and munitions to American cruisers and by helping stranded and captive American sailors, as well as American businessmen who were having financial difficulties in Europe, he exposed himself to the wrath of the British government. The British pressured the court of Lisbon, which banished Dohrmann from Portugal in 1782. He left his business and extensive banking interests in the hands of a brother and departed for New York. On July 9, 1785, Washington wrote a letter to the Honorable Samuel Chase recommending Dohrman,

> who at an early period of the war (when our affairs were rather overshadowed) advanced his money very liberally to support our suffering countrymen in captivity. He has some matter to submit to Congress which he can explain better than I. I am persuaded he will offer nothing which is inconsistent with the strictest rules of propriety and of course that it will merit your patronage.

On the report of the treasurer, Congress made the following resolutions on behalf of Dohrmann:

Whereas the claims of Arnold Henry Dohrmann against the United States of America amounted to $20,277 over and above the sum of $5,806, as above stated, in support of which important documents are offered by Mr. Dohrmann, whose own house was frequently the asylum of whole crews of captive American seamen, who were fed, clothed, and relieved in sickness through his benevolence, that at a time when his attachment to the cause of America was dangerous both to his person and property.

And whereas Congress are disposed to acknowledge in the most honorable manner the eminent services rendered by Mr. Dohrmann and make him further compensation:

Resolved unanimously: that the said A. H. Dohrmann be allowed, as agent from the United States at the Court of Lisbon, the sum of $1600 per annum, and that said salary be computed from that period at which his expenditures commenced to the present day.

Resolved unanimously: That one complete and entire township . . . surveyed in the western territory of the United States, be granted to A. H. Dohrmann, free from all charges of survey, and with choice of the three ranges last surveyed.[19]

These resolutions were entered Monday, October 1, 1787, in the *Journal of Congress* (vol. IV, p. 784). On December 18, 1787, Arnold Henry Dohrmann, born in Hamburg, became a naturalized citizen of the United States. In 1789 Dohrmann survived the financial crash at Lisbon. With the help of James Madison and Thomas Jefferson as his lawyers, he was able to pay his debts; but the loss of three ships in 1808 broke his fortunes. He had to sell the land given to him by Congress, and he died a broken man in 1813 at Steubenville, Ohio. Congress voted a pension for his wife in 1817.

A daring attempt to help the American cause was successfully made by John Paul Schott, formerly an officer in the service of Frederick the Second, king of Prussia. In early 1776, Schott had arrived in New York to offer his military services to the British. He changed his mind, however, when he learned more about the cause of the American colonists. Observing their lack of guns and ammunition, he put his money into a daring enterprise to provide the needed supplies. In the summer of 1776 he went to St. Eustache, an island of the Lesser Antilles where the Dutch had established a station loaded with goods and contraband of war. Schott hired a schooner, loaded it with weapons and ammunition and steered for the coast of Virginia. Having dressed his entire crew in the uniform of English sailors and hoisting a British flag, he deceived the English fleet which was blockading the entrance to Hampton Roads. The schooner was fired upon by the colonists as it approached Norfolk, because the crew did not have the time to remove the British uniforms. When Schott hoisted a white flag, the schooner anchored safely in the harbor. The Americans gladly bought the sorely needed supplies.

Soon afterward Schott's petition for an officer's rank in the Continental army was granted. Captain Schott joined General Washington for active service at New York. At the battle of White Plains he commanded the Third Battery in Colonel Knox's artillery. On July 31, 1777, Washington sent Schott to Pennsylvania to recruit an independent troop of German dragoons. He had permission to appoint his own officers and to give commands in German. Three more companies were later placed under his command. At the battle of Short Hills he was severely wounded and taken prisoner while covering the retreat. The British offered him a position in their army; but Schott refused, as he explained later in a letter to the Honorable Richard Rush on June 28, 1828, "I had chosen America as my fatherland, and nothing could induce me to desert her just cause." After a prisoner exchange in 1779, Schott again served in the army, commanding the right wing in the brigade of General Hand under General Sullivan. Both generals recommended Schott for promotion. But the wounds received in the battle of Short Hills made active service more difficult for him. He was, therefore, placed in command of the forts in Wyoming, Pennsylvania, serving in that position to the end of the war. He was credited with a lifelong annual pension of $1,200 in the pension lists of 1828.

Many more German names fill the early military and pension lists of the United States, testifying to the degree that German efforts and heroism helped to win independence for the colonists.

Both before and during the War of Independence, courageous trappers and hunters continued to move westward. In this enterprise they became the "rearguard of the Revolution." Since many early German settlements were eventually located along the western frontier, it is not surprising that many Germans were among the pioneers of the West. Germans formed a good part of George Rogers Clark's force which captured the British forts north of the Ohio River. The British officers of these forts had encouraged the Indians to attack white settlements. To stop these attacks, Clark wanted to take the British forts by surprise and persuaded Patrick Henry, governor of Virginia, to support his plan. To avoid weakening the seaboard people in their revolutionary struggle, Patrick Henry ordered that the companies be raised from backwoods riflemen west of the Blue Ridge. Thus, many men were chosen from the German population of the Valley of Virginia.

Clark crossed the Appalachian Mountains in May 1778 with his small force of about one hundred eighty men. Two of the captains of this expeditionary force were of German descent, Joseph Bowman (Baumann) and Leonard Helm. Captain Bowman received the surrender of Fort Cahokia, and Captain Helm became commander of the captured Fort Vincennes. Since Clark did not receive any reinforcements, British Colonel Henry Hamilton succeeded in recapturing Fort Vincennes, where he settled for the winter of 1778-1779. But Clark did not give up the fight. He gathered his depleted forces at Kaskaskia and began the march of two hundred fifty miles across the half-frozen prairies to Vincennes.

Joseph Bowman was the commander of one of the companies trying to reconquer Vincennes. The brief notes in Bowman's diary give us a good picture of this brave campaign:

> The road very bad from the immense quantity of rain that had fallen. The men much fatigued.... Marched all day thro' rain and water. Our provisions began to be short.

... Many of the men much cast down, particularly the volunteers.... Camp very quiet but hungry; some almost in despair.... Our pilots say we cannot get along—that it is impossible.... Heard the morning and evening guns from the fort. No provisions yet. Lord, help us! ... Set off to cross the Horse-Shoe plain about four miles long all covered with water breast high. Here we expected some of our brave men must certainly perish, having froze in the night and so long fasting. Having no other resource than wading this plain or rather lake of waters we plunged into it with courage. Never were men so animated with the thought of avenging the wrongs done the back settlements as this small army was.[20]

On February 23, 1779, this handful of frozen, starving men attacked the fort, and after a short siege, Hamilton surrendered the fort to Clark. Captain Helm was set free and continued to serve under Clark. Sent on a mission to Aux Miami, the present site of Fort Wayne, he captured seven boats loaded with provisions. While the enemy prisoners were sent by boat to Kaskaskia, Helm was placed in command of the town and dealt with all civil matters.

18
The War of 1812

The War of 1812, the last war the United States fought against England, is sometimes called the Second War of Independence, but it was actually a most unpopular war. The New York militia, for instance, refused to support the regular army in its attempt to take Canada in 1812. When General Henry Dearborn tried an assault against Montreal, his soldiers simply would not cross the border on the grounds that they had not signed up to fight beyond it. In spite of many setbacks, especially by the American land forces, there were a few brilliant feats to which soldiers of German blood contributed. Thus, the credit for saving the artillery at Chrystler's field on the St. Lawrence River belongs to General Walbach, who was born in Muenster, Germany, in 1766. In that battle the American army under General Wilkinson suffered severely, losing 339 of its best officers and men, while the British lost 187. Walbach had come to the United States in 1798 after a distinguished career in the French, Austrian, and British military. For his bravery in battle at Chrystler's field he was promoted to brigadier general and to commander of the Fourth Artillery, U.S. Army.

In 1814 the British took the city of Washington. Of the

ninety-five thousand Americans who had been called up to defend the city, only seven thousand had shown up. President Madison and his wife, Dolly, had been forced to depart in haste, taking only a few papers, some silver, Stuart's portrait of Washington, and Dolly's parrot. The British officers arrived in time to enjoy the supper which had been prepared for the president's party, while British troops burned down Washington in retaliation for the burning of York (present-day Toronto) by American troops in 1813. Alerted by the dismal fate of Washington, the citizens of Baltimore were prepared, and the British attempt to capture Baltimore was stopped. Fort McHenry at the sea entrance of the harbor was provided with ample ammunition, and all militia companies were in arms and ready to march. When news arrived that the enemy was approaching in seventy ships and had landed a force of seven thousand soldiers, three thousand militia-men under the command of the German-American general John Stricker went out immediately to retard the attack. The American forces slowly yielded to an enemy superior in number and experience. It was the shot of a sharpshooter that broke up the attack by fatally wounding the British commander, General Ross, who died on the way back to the ships.

General John Stricker was born in Frederick, Maryland, in 1759, the son of Colonel George Stricker of Revotionary fame. Stricker had served as a cadet in the German battalion of which his father was lieutenant colonel, and had taken part in the battles of Trenton, Princeton, Brandywine, Germantown, Monmouth, and others. He also had accompanied General Sullivan in his expeditions against the Indians. In 1783 he became a captain and settled in Baltimore, where he formed and trained one of the earliest militia commands. He soon was promoted to brigadier general and commander of the state's troops.

While General John Stricker and his militia-men thwarted the British land attack, a German-Virginian withstood bombardment by sixteen British war vessels which lasted for thirty-six hours. He was General George Armistead, born in 1780 at New Market, Virginia. The British landed a force of about one thousand men to attack the fort from the rear. Major Armistead and his men drove them back, and it was during this fierce battle that Francis Scott Key, while a prisoner aboard a British ship, wrote "The Star-Spangled Banner."

George Armistead was promoted to lieutenant colonel after his successful defense of Fort McHenry. During the War of 1812 five of George's brothers served in the army, three with the regulars and two with the militia. Walter Keith Armistead, born in 1785, was engineer and superintendent of the fortifications at Norfolk, Virginia, and was appointed director general.

The Armistead family is among the most distinguished families in the history of Virginia. Robert Armistead's grandfather had come from Hessen-Darmstadt, Germany. His daughter was President John Tyler's mother. From a letter by Mrs. Letitia Tyler Semple, daughter of President Tyler, to George G. Vest, U. S. senator from Missouri, we learn that the Armisteads were related to four U. S. presidents. In a letter from Louisenheim, Washington, D. C., dated April 20, Mrs. Semple writes, "James Monroe, William Henry Harrison, John Tyler, and Benjamin Harrison are cousins, being related with the Armisteads and Tylers of Virginia."[1]

The Baltimore Germans had a full company of "Jaeger"[2] on the battlefields of the War of 1812, and the Pennsylvania Germans contributed their full share of soldiers to the war. The service-in-war record of three Pennsylvania German families serve as noteworthy examples. The Pennypacker family had five members in the Revolutionary War and three in the Mexican War; in the War of 1812 it had two members in the field. Their ancestor, Heinrich Pennypacker, had come from Germany and settled sometime before 1699 on Skippack Creek. The Muehlenberg family was represented by at least six members on the registers of the regular army during the nineteenth century. Finally, members of the Hambright family distinguished themselves not only during the Revolutionary War but also during the War of 1812; Frederick Hambright served as a major general of the militia, and his brother George was a colonel.

19
The Mexican War

The Mexican War officially began on May 13, 1846, though it had actually started in 1836, when the settlers of Texas defied Santa Anna's dictatorship and declared their independence after their decisive victory at San Jacinto on April 21, 1836. A son of a German Lutheran minister, General John A. Quitman, organized a group of recruits at his own expense to help General Houston, but his group was delayed by marauders and other problems along the way. When Quitman and his contingent joined General Houston, they were too late; the battle of San Jacinto had just been fought.

Quitman made up for this later by being the first one to enter Mexico City with his troops when the city fell on September 14, 1847. All during the Mexican War he had been one of the most daring generals under General Taylor. He commanded a brigade, and attacked Monterey with General Worth. At Alvarado he was in command and he led the assault on Vera Cruz. The storming of Fort Chapultepec, which was well defended, was due largely to the bravery of Quitman and his men. After they successfully attacked the Belen Gate, Mexico City was evacuated during the night.

With his exhausted, tattered troops General Quitman was the first to enter the Grand Plaza of the city. Many American soldiers were wounded and half-clothed; Quitman himself wore only one shoe when he rode into the city. Quitman was appointed governor of Mexico City by General Scott, and in later years he served as governor of Mississippi and as congressman. He died in 1858.

Many other officers who were native Germans or of German descent made names for themselves. Among these was James Lawson Kemper, a Virginian German and later governor of the state from 1873 to 1878, who served as captain of a company of volunteers. Also as a captain, Samuel P. Heintzelman, a graduate of West Point, distinguished himself during the Mexican War, which prepared him for greater successes later during the Civil War. Captain Henry Koch and General August V. Kautz, both born in Germany, served with distinction in the Mexican War.

German-Americans were among the first to volunteer at the outbreak of the Mexican War. The first volunteers from St. Louis were Germans. The towns of St. Charles and Hermann in Missouri sent a good-sized contingent of soldiers. A German raised the first company for service in Kentucky, and over six hundred Germans volunteered in New Orleans. The first regiment organized in Cincinnati was also German. In Texas and Missouri Germans filled the state cavalry and artillery companies. In Illinois, J. C. Raith and Adolph Engelmann commanded a company raised by Germans from Belleville.

When President Polk declared war on Mexico, Germans in general did not hesitate to take up arms even though most Germans were against slavery and realized that the slaveholders would gain most by the war, which stripped Mexico of two-fifths of her territory. After the war against Mexico, Germans continued to be opponents of slavery, a fact they demonstrated during the Civil War.

20
The Civil War

The statistical work by B. A. Gould, *Investigations in the Military and Anthropological Statistics of American Soldiers* (New York, 1869), states that the number of foreign-born German volunteers in the Civil War exceeded the number of Irish by 32,596. The Irish sent 5,169 in excess of the general average, while the Germans topped this by sending 28,596 men in excess of the general average. These interesting statistics illustrate the significant participation of both these groups. Other facts indicate the distinction earned by men of German blood during the Civil War. Of the six major generalships bestowed on men of foreign birth, four went to Germans—Franz Sigel, Carl Schurz, Peter Joseph Osterhaus, and Adolf von Steinwehr. In addition, nine Germans were promoted to brigadier general and a great number became colonels. German-born volunteers in the Civil War numbered 176,817. A conservative estimate of volunteers of German stock who served in the northern armies amounts to about five hundred thousand, which includes the 176,817 born in Germany.

There is no doubt among historians that the German element in Missouri contributed decisively to keeping this

border state within the Union. A United States arsenal
located within the city of St. Louis held the key to whether
the state would go to the North or to the South. John B.
Floyd, prosecession secretary of war, had filled the arsenal
to overflowing with arms and ammunition, expecting that it
would be taken by the Southerners. Moreover, C. F. Jackson,
governor of Missouri, sympathized with the Southern cause.
President Lincoln informed Jackson on April 14, 1861, that
his state's quota of volunteers for three months' service in
the Federal army would be four thousand troops. The governor immediately replied, "Your requisition is illegal, un-
constitutional, and revolutionary in its object, inhuman and
diabolical, and cannot be complied with."[1] A few days later
Governor Jackson's state troops took possession of government supplies at Liberty. If it had not been for Captain
Lyon, commander of the St. Louis arsenal, Francis P. Blair,
congressman and editor of the Republican newspaper, the
St. Louis Democrat, and the German citizens, the St. Louis
arsenal would have fallen into the hands of the secessionist
militia, the so-called Minute Men. The Minute Men, encouraged by the successful capture of arms at Liberty, wanted to
take the arsenal at St. Louis. Though Mayor Taylor of St.
Louis was prosecession, he warned the Minute Men against
using force, fearing bloodshed between them and the German
home guard and Turner Society militia. The latter had received military training by an officer of the United States
Army, E. D. Larned. At this threat by the Minute Men, the
Germans insisted on being admitted to the arsenal to be
armed, so they would be able to keep St. Louis and Missouri
effectively within the Union. Without waiting for Washington's approval, Captain Lyon allowed the German volunteers to enter the arsenal on April 22. Five regiments were
formed and armed; and all were commanded by Germans
except the first regiment, which was commanded by F. P.
Blair. As well as arming their own men, Blair and Lyon dispatched thirty thousand muskets and ten thousand pounds
of powder to Illinois to arm the volunteer regiments there.

As a countermove, Governor Jackson placed seven hundred members of the state militia into a camp at Lindell

Grove outside St. Louis. Camp Jackson, as it was called, was
taken without bloodshed by Lyon and his troops on May
10. General Frost, the secessionist commander of Camp Jackson, surrendered under protest. The Jackson forces were
disarmed and marched under heavy guard to the arsenal
where they were to be given their paroles. Along the route
a large crowd hostile to the Union forces had gathered,
shouting "damn Dutch blackguards," "long-eared Dutchmen," and "mercenary Hessians."² If Captain Lyon's horse
had not suddenly bolted and thrown Lyon to the ground discipline would yet have been preserved. When the column
of guards and prisoners halted, the onlooking mob tried to cut
through the guards. Someone in the crowd fired a revolver
and hit Captain Blandowsky, a Polish-German. As if a signal
had been given, a crowd attacked with clubs and stones.
The troops opened fire immediately, without waiting for an
order. Before the shooting came to an end two militiamen
and twenty-six rioters were dead and many more wounded.

The grave situation in St. Louis was kept from worse
violence as the five German regiments discouraged any
retaliatory action by the Minute Men and other secessionists.
General Harney, who was friendly to Governor Jackson,
was removed by an order of the War Department. Captain
Lyon was promoted to brigadier general, St. Louis remained
firmly in the hands of the Union. In retrospect, General
Grant described the situation as a key factor in the Union
position at the beginning of the war:

> There was some splendid work done in Missouri, and
> especially in St. Louis, in the earliest days of the war,
> which people have now almost forgotten. If St. Louis would
> have been captured by the rebels it would have been a
> terrible task to recapture St. Louis—one of the most diffi-
> cult that could have been given to any military man. In-
> stead of a campaign before Vicksburg, it would have been
> a campaign before St. Louis.³

The Germans contributed about five hundred officers
with the rank of major, colonel, or general to the Union
armies; ninety-six of them gave their lives. For a time two

generals of German descent occupied leading positions in
the Union army. California German "Old Brains" Halleck,
who replaced General McClellan as general in chief, was a
West Point graduate. Another graduate of West Point, General William S. Rosencrans, commanded the Cumberland
army. He was from a German Catholic family of Ohio (his
brother was bishop of Cincinnati) and was known by the
nickname "Old Rosy." General August V. Kautz, who had
served as a lieutenant in the Mexican War, distinguished
himself in the Civil War as chief of cavalry of the Twenty-
Third Corps and was noted for his cavalry raids in southern
Virginia during 1864. He also commanded the first troops of
black Americans. Another veteran of the Mexican War,
General S. P. Heintzelman, commanded the Northern Department in 1863. His grandfather had come from Augsburg,
Germany, and had been the first white settler in Manheim,
Pennsylvania.

Germans who had taken part in the ill-fated German
revolution of 1848 and who later had immigrated to America,
rendered important service in the Civil War. The Forty-
Eighters became prominent in many professional fields after
they crossed the ocean to accomplish their dreams and ideals
in the United States. As journalists and politicians they
managed to win the support of the sometimes reluctant German-American population for the cause of the Union. Franz
Sigel, hero of the insurrection of Baden, Germany, was
already known to German-Americans for his skillful retreat
into Switzerland against an overpowering Prussian army
without losing a man or any piece of artillery. The insurrec-
tionary government of Baden had appointed him minister
of war, but the revolution failed, and Sigel had to leave
neutral Switzerland. By 1857, Sigel was teaching in St.
Louis at the German American Institute.

When President Lincoln issued the call to arms in April
of 1861, Sigel immediately organized the Third Missouri
Volunteers, one of the first regiments in the state. His name
worked like magic on German civilians and the phrase "I
fights mit Sigel" induced thousands of German-Americans
to volunteer their service for the cause of the Union. Much

controversy clouds Sigel's performance as a military leader during the Civil War. Nevertheless, his contributions to the victory of the North are well summed up in the *Dictionary of American Biography*, "A love for free government had been the ruling motive of Sigel's life. His military successes were not of the greatest, but his prompt and ardent espousal of the Union cause was a great factor in uniting the large German population of the North, with which he was extremely popular, solidly behind the Union."

Another Forty-Eighter who took to the cause of the Union with great enthusiasm was Carl Schurz. On October 3, 1863, Schurz wrote to his friend Theodor Petrasch,

> What a tremendous problem and what a mighty cause! I am happy to live in this country at this time. In comparison with the splendid goal, what are our little sufferings and individual sacrifices? Slavery is being driven out of its last citadel; the insulted dignity of human nature is being avenged. The people of the new world are taking an immeasurable step forward in its cleansing and ennobling.

Schurz let his deed follow his words. He could safely have remained in Spain as ambassador during the Civil War, but he asked President Lincoln again and again for a military command. When he was finally given a generalship, Schurz proved himself a capable military leader in spite of his minimal military training. The tribute paid to Schurz by Colonel Leopold von Gilsa seems to have been justified, "General, I owe you an apology. When you were appointed brigadier, I regarded you as a mere civilian and indulged in some hard language. I want to say in the opinion of everybody you have fully earned your rank, and I have come to pay you my profound respects."[5]

Schurz demonstrated his skill in many battles—outstanding was the second battle of Bull Run, where his division sustained bitter struggle for eight hours and was still able to cover a successful retreat. Critics of Schurz accused him of being vainglorious in seeking military service. Schurz's reason for entering the military struggle was simply stated in a letter to his friend Petrasch, dated September 24, 1863, "I belonged to the party that brought on the crisis; I could not avoid the chances of the struggle. . . . Then I will return to my old activities with the satisfaction not only of having labored definitively for the future of the country, but also of having loyally shared its fate."[6]

Peter Joseph Osterhaus rose from private to the rank of major general, the only higher rank being that of lieutenant general, which was reserved for Grant. Osterhaus had received somewhat limited military training in Berlin, and his participation in the Baden Revolution of 1848-1849 had motivated his flight to the United States. At the outbreak of the Civil War he enlisted as a volunteer in the Second Missouri Regiment. On account of his previous military experience, he was soon promoted to major, commanding a battalion of the Second Missouri Regiment. In December 1861, he advanced to the rank of colonel in charge of the Twelfth Missouri Regiment. During the battle of Pea Ridge, March 1862, Osterhaus commanded one of Sigel's two divisions and stormed the enemy's main position at Eldhorn Pass. This success led to his promotion to brigadier general the following June.

The battle of Lookout Mountain made him a hero. Osterhaus asked General Hooker for the assignment of attacking the mountain position. When, toward evening, the Union flag was seen unfurled at the top of Lookout Mountain by the men at Grant's headquarters, one of the staff said, "That's the work of 'Fighting Joe,' " meaning Hooker. Grant shook his head and said, "I don't think it is 'Fighting Joe,' I think it's 'Peter Joe.' "[7] Osterhaus was promoted to major general before he participated in the campaign of Atlanta under Sherman. Osterhaus was in no less than thirty-four battles; he was never defeated when allowed to lead his troops independently. General Sherman paid high tribute to Osterhaus in regard to the three day battle around Chattanooga, saying, "I left one of my best divisions, that of Osterhaus, to act with Hooker, and I know it has served the country well and reflected honor to the Army of the Tennessee."

August von Willich was another German-American who

rose to the rank of general. At age twelve he entered the cadet school at Potsdam and afterward attended the Berlin military academy. A captain of artillery at the age of thirty, his military career in Germany came to a sudden end because he favored communistic ideas directed against the government. When the army accepted his resignation, he became a carpenter, which made him an outcast to his family and relatives. It was by that time inevitable that Willich would take part in the Baden Revolution. Upon its failure, he fled first to Switzerland and then to England, where he joined one of the most radical clubs. Willich's idealistic communism brought him the ridicule of Karl Marx for being the "knight of noble conviction" and a "spiritual communist."

When Willich first arrived at New York in 1853, he again worked as a carpenter. By the start of the Civil War he had moved to Cincinnati, and had become editor of a workingman's paper, the *Deutsche Republikaner*. At the president's call for volunteers he promptly joined the Ninth Ohio Regiment, becoming its drillmaster. As a major with the Ninth Ohio, he participated in the West Virginia campaign. Later, when Governor Morton of Indiana was looking for someone to organize a German regiment and offered Willich the job with the rank of colonel, Willich accepted. Within a month he drilled the Thirty-Second Indiana Regiment into a brilliant fighting unit, which maneuvered by trumpet signals, in the Prussian style. In his *Autobiography* General Lew Wallace described the conduct of Willich's regiment in the Battle of Shiloh as follows:

> They were but a regiment; yet at the sight of them the enemy halted, about faced and returned to his position in the woods. There he struck out with fire so lively that the newcomers halted and showed signs of distress. Then an officer rode swiftly around their left flank and stopped when in front of them, his back to the enemy. What he said I could not hear, but from the motions of the men he was putting them through the manual of arms—this notwithstanding that some of them were dropping in the ranks. Taken all in all, *that* I think was the most audacious thing that came under my observation during the war. The effect

was magical. The colonel returned to his post in the rear, and the regiment steadied as if on parade, advancing in the face of the fire pouring upon them and actually entered the wood.

On my part, then, no time was lost pressing the division forward; and while the order was in delivery I dispatched an orderly to the colonel of the unknown regiment with my compliments and asked his name. "August Willich of the Thirty-Second Indiana Volunteers," was the reply brought me.[8]

For his brilliant service at Shiloh, Willich was promoted to brigadier general. He repeated the daring procedure described above at Perryville and Chickamauga, succeeding always to steady his men to continue the fighting. From April 1861 to February 1864 he served uninterruptedly in the Union army. In the battle of Resaca in May 1864, he received a severe bullet wound in his shoulder, which incapacitated him for further active service. He was made commander of the Cincinnati military district. Willich had been in more than thirty battles, and when his corps mustered out in October 1865, he was accorded the brevet rank of major general as his final recognition.

Adolph von Steinwehr was the fourth German-born soldier to advance to the rank of major general. He had taken part in the Mexican War, and when the Civil War broke out, he recruited a regiment of volunteers in New York. As the Twenty-Ninth Regiment of New York it became part of Blenker's Brigade and stood its ground at the stone bridge and slope west of Centerville in the battle of Bull Run when others fled stricken with panic. Though he took part in many other battles, Adolph von Steinwehr distinguished himself most in the battle of Gettysburg. It was he who pointed out the strategic importance of Cemetery Ridge to General Howard and advised to entrench there instead of advancing against the enemy. Referring to Steinwehr's services, General Howard said, "I must speak of General Steinwehr. He came upon the field with a hearty spirit, ready to do his part. During the retreat he kept his men steadily in position on Cemetery Ridge as a nucleus, on which the line of battle, probably the most important in the annals of our war, was formed."[9] On July 3, 1863, it was on Cemetery Ridge that the Union forces successfully withstood the attack of fifteen thousand rebels known as "Pickett's charge."

J. F. Rhodes, historian of the Civil War, reports a part of Pickett's charge as follows:

> In the last assault, Armistead, a brigade commander, leaped the stone wall, waved his sword with his hat on it, shouted, "Give them the cold steel, boys," and laid his hands upon a gun. A hundred of his men had followed. They planted the Confederate battle flags on Cemetery Ridge among the cannon they had captured, and for a moment held. Armistead was shot down; Garnett and Kemper, Pickett's other brigadiers, fell. The wavering divisions of Hill's corps seemed appalled, broke their ranks, and fell back.[10]

General L. A. Armistead and General James L. Kemper mentioned in the report above were men of German descent who fought for the Confederacy. L. A. Armistead was a Mexican War veteran and had served in the Indian War in Florida under his father, General W. K. Armistead. The Armistead family had had a long record of military service. George Armistead, mentioned earlier as the defender of Fort McHenry against the British fleet in 1814, was a member of this family.

General Kemper descended from one of the oldest settlers in Virginia. His forefather had settled in Germanna under the auspices of Governor Spotswood. Armistead was killed at Pickett's charge, and Kemper was severely wounded. As soon as he recovered, Kemper was placed in command of the forces at Richmond, later becoming governor of the state of Virginia from 1873 to 1878.

The early German settlers in the South were not surprisingly in favor of the Confederate cause. Though most of them were opposed to slavery, they had become accustomed to the Southern way of life. It is estimated that more than ten thousand Germans served in the Confederate army; and they served valiantly, as the examples of Armistead and

Kemper show. Many more Germans advanced to the rank of commander, as the records of names such as Wagener, Backmann, Buchholz, Eichholz, Kolb, and Reichard attest. Karl Gustav Memminger, who had come from Germany to America as a child, was slated to become secretary of the treasury in case of a Confederate victory.

One of the most colorful officers in the army of the South was Major Heros von Borcke. General Lee called him the "German Goliath" because of his enormous height and weight. He was extremely popular with his men and fellow officers, especially because he knew how to entertain them with theatrical performances. His shadow plays were unsurpassed and very successful. He was equally successful on the battlefield, serving as major of the cavalry on Jeb Stuart's staff. He was severely wounded in the battle of Chancellorsville. After he had recovered from his wounds, von Borcke returned to Germany, where he participated in the Prussian-Austrian war of 1866. He reentered the United States in 1884 and settled in Baltimore. Whenever old friends from the war visited him, he flew the flags of Prussia and the Confederacy next to each other from the tower of a small castle he had built for himself.

Many more pages could be filled with the deeds of German-Americans on both sides of the battle line during the Civil War, but they are well summarized in the words of A. B. Faust, "That the Germans were superior to all others they never attempted to claim, but they can furnish abundant proof of having fought as bravely and steadily on the great battlefields of the Civil War as any other national element."[11]

21
The Spanish-American War

The Spanish-American War eliminated Spain's rule in the "front yard of the United States," the Philippines, Puerto Rico, and Cuba. On April 11, 1889, President McKinley sent a message to Congress asking for "forcible intervention" on account of the continuous disturbances on the part of Spain which "caused enormous losses to American trade and commerce, caused irritation, annoyance, and disturbance among our citizens, and by the exercise of cruel, barbarous, and uncivilized practices of warfare, shocked the sensibilities and offended the sympathies of our people." Congress approved the resolution to "secure a full and final termination of hostilities between the government of Spain and the people of Cuba." When the State Department communicated the information to the Spanish government, Spain declared war on April 24, 1898.

The spark which had ignited this powderkeg was the sinking of the U. S. battleship *Maine*, which had been sent to Havana to protect American lives and property. On February 15, 1898, and explosion sent the ship to the bottom of the harbor and two hundred and sixty men to their death. Among the dead were twenty-one sailors of German blood.

There were many others who were to give their service and their lives for their country in the war that followed.

Theodor Schwan, with a long service record in the U. S. Army, crowned his military career as brigadier general in the Spanish-American War. He commanded the army which marched against Mayaguez on the west coast of Puerto Rico and fought a bloody battle on August 10, 1898, at Hormigueros against strong Spanish resistance. In the Philippines, Schwan was in charge of the expeditions in the province of Cavite and in Southern Luzon. John Walter Clous (also spelled Klaus) was also promoted to brigadier general for his distinguished service as staff officer under General Miles. General Physician George M. Sternberg was responsible for the entire medical corps.

Perhaps the most prominent service rendered during the Spanish-American War was that of Admiral Winfield Scott Schley. He was a descendant of a schoolmaster, Thomas Schley, who had built the first house in Frederick, Maryland, in 1735. Admiral Schley was in command of the American fleet at Santiago, Cuba, when Spanish Admiral Cervera tried to break through the American blockade on July 3, 1898. The entire Spanish fleet was destroyed, and the war was, in effect, ended. While the Spanish navy had suffered six hundred casualties, only one dead and one wounded on the American side made Schley's victory even more impressive. Two thousand prisoners, among them Admiral Cervera, fell into the hands of the American forces. When, on July 17, the city of Santiago capitulated, an additional twenty-two thousand prisoners were taken, and four hundred years of Spanish dominion over the coastal islands had ended.

22
World Wars I and II

With the advent of World War I, the German-American community was caught in the middle and was to suffer many traumatic experiences. Most German-Americans hoped that the struggle would be fought out among the European powers, and some sought actively to keep the United States neutral. But neutrality proved to be impossible. President Wilson's sympathies were clearly with the Allies. His trusted adviser, Colonel E. M. House, was already trying in 1913 to bring about a sympathetic alliance between Britain and the United States. And when in December of 1915, the minister of the United States to Belgium remarked to Wilson, "I ought to tell you that in my heart there is no such thing as neutrality; I am heart and soul for the Allies," Wilson replied, "So am I. No decent man, knowing the situation in Germany, could be anything else." So there were good guys and bad guys, as Walter Millis wrote (approximately twenty years later) in *The Road to War: America 1914-1917*:

When prominent Germans, like Kuno Francke or Professor Muensterberg of Harvard, leapt to perform for the German cause the service which Lord Bryce and so many other prominent Britons were performing for the Allies, they were shocked and hurt by the indifference with which their activities were regarded. When eminent Americans of German ancestry like the Ridders in New York defended the Central Powers with the same passion which innumerable other Americans were bringing to the support of the Entente, they were dismayed to find that in their case such efforts were held to be akin to treason.[1]

The bungled attempts of the imperial government of Germany to stir up trouble in Mexico against the United States and all the efforts of the German-American press to keep the United States out of the war actually accentuated the American sentiment against Germany and her allies. Emotional involvement in the war was soon followed by economic aid to the Allies. Robert Marion La Follette, senator from Wisconsin, was (in spite of his French ancestry) against American involvement, and wrote in September 1915:

> With the first clash of the Great European War came President Wilson's solemn appeal... "The United States must be neutral in fact as well as name."... But when you can boom stocks 600 percent in manufacturing munitions—to the Bottomless Pit with Neutrality! What do Morgan and Schwab care for world peace when there are big profits in world war?... The stocks of the Schwab properties which stood at a market value of seven million before they began supplying the Allies... are today given an "aggregate value" of forty-nine million. And now we are about to engage in furnishing the Allies funds.... We have ceased to be "neutral in fact as well as in name."[2]

About one year later, in August of 1916, a $500 million Anglo-French loan was floated. Approximately $2.3 billion had been loaned to the Allies up to the time of the United States' entry into the war; Germany had received a much smaller loan of $27 million. It was of no avail that "Fighting Bob" La Follette thundered from the Senate floor:

> I had supposed until recently that it was the duty of senators and representatives in Congress to vote and act

according to their convictions. Quite another doctrine has recently been promulgated...and that is the doctrine of "standing back of the president" without inquiring whether the president is right or wrong. For myself, I have never subscribed to that doctrine and never shall....[3]

For hours La Follette filibustered against American intervention, but when it came to a vote only six senators were against a declaration of war. On April 6, the House followed the affirmative vote of the Senate, with fifty members voting against it.

Immediately upon declaration of war, the overwhelming majority of the German-American community recognized only one loyalty—the one toward the United States. The German-American general who led the American expeditionary forces to France in 1917 was John J. Pershing, whose ancestor Frederick Pfoerschin (the name later anglicized to Pershing) had landed in Philadelphia on October 2, 1749. After Frederick had worked as a bond servant for five years, he had moved to Westmoreland County, where he acquired his own farm and married Mari Elizabeth Weygandt. The Pfoerschin family spread over the entire United States as General Pershing, Frederick's famous great-grandson, wrote:

Each generation furnished pioneers as the frontier moved westward. They were found in the columns that settled the Western Reserve; in the trains that carried civilization to Indiana, Illinois, Missouri, and the Middle West, and were represented among the early settlers of Oregon and California. Their log cabins have dotted every state from Pennsylvania to the Pacific.[4]

The family history relates a story about Conrad, one of Frederick Pfoerschin's sons, who became a Lutheran pastor and accompanied a retaliative expedition against the Indians at Fort Liggonier in 1792. As the story goes, Reverend Conrad insisted on leading the militia company into prayer just before the attack. He prayed with such a loud voice that the Indians became alarmed and took to their heels. When reading the story General Pershing scrawled rather dryly in the margin, "Hardly a military proceeding."

By contrast, Pershing's own war-time record was highly military as well as successful. The earliest engagement of the American First Army was at Saint-Mihiel in September of 1918. The victory was followed up by Pershing and his 1.2 million "doughboys" with the Meuse-Argonne campaign, which brought Germany to its knees. Early in 1918, before the bulk of the American expeditionary forces had been committed to action, the Thirty-Second Division was sent to the Vosges Mountains for combat duty although some staff officers had questioned the division's reliability. The Thirty-Second was mainly composed of National Guard troops from Wisconsin and Michigan with many German-Americans in their ranks. But General Pershing trusted his fellow German-Americans, who fought bravely and made the Thirty-Second one of the crack divisions of the A.E.F. It was probably one of the greatest days in the history of Milwaukee, when, on June 6, 1919, the Thirty-Second Division marched down Grand (now Wisconsin) Avenue, because it meant the end of all the sneers and excesses which a super-patriotism had hurled at the German-American community. "Black Jack" Pershing was made general of the armies in 1919, a position previously held only by George Washington. In 1932 General Pershing won a Pulitzer Prize for his book, *My Experiences in the World War*. He died in July 1948.

There was strong feeling and eagerness in the German-American community to do even more than was expected to prove their loyalty to America. For the First Liberty Loan Drive, Milwaukee's quota was set at $14 million. Milwaukee exceeded this sum by $4 million.

Another example of going "beyond the call of duty" was the two-man team of American combat fliers, Joseph Wehner and Frank Luke, who were both of German ancestry. Major Harold Hartney, their commanding officer, described the way the two young men met for the first time, as quoted in Arch Whitehouse's *The Year of the Sky Kings*:

Luke walked in just as I was reassuring Joe Wehner

that he had nothing to worry about. Because of his name some over-anxious Intelligence operator had been hounding the boy and he was not happy about it. A funny thing, as he walked out he and Luke exchanged just a hint of a grin. I didn't know it then but in that brief encounter was born one of the greatest fighting teams the U. S. Air Service was to inscribe in its records.[5]

The team of Luke and Wehner became very successful in shooting down German observation balloons and destroying enemy planes. Lieutenant Wehner was Luke's wingman, and provided air cover, while Frank concentrated on shooting down the gasbags. With Wehner covering, Luke shot down four German planes and fifteen observation balloons on ten combat patrols. This feat made Luke famous in the United States, and newspaper headlines celebrated him as "The Balloon Buster." When Wehner was shot down, Luke could think only of revenging his partner. He became a brooding loner who departed on unauthorized solo flights, of which one was to be fatal to him. On September 29, 1918, Luke shot down an enemy balloon, and was then shot down himself by German fighter planes. He survived the crash landing outside the French village of Murvaus, but as witnesses relate:

> [Luke] apparently wounded by a shot fired from a rapid-fire cannon ... got out of his machine. ... He had gone about fifty yards when, seeing the Germans come toward him, he still had strength to draw his revolver to defend himself, and a moment after he fell dead, following a serious wound received in the chest.[6]

Frank Luke was the first U. S. airman to receive the Congressional Medal of Honor; and Luke Field in Hawaii is named after him.

Edward V. Rickenbacker (originally Richenbacher) became the greatest American hero of the air. He was credited with shooting down twenty-two enemy planes and four observation balloons. At first he was considered too old at twenty-six and was rejected when he applied for the army flying school. For this reason he went to France in 1917 as a chauffeur on General Pershing's staff. He later convinced General Billy Mitchell to admit him for aerial training. Eddie became a member and later the commander of the famed 94th Aero Squadron, the leading American flying team of World War I. He reached the rank of major and was showered with American and French war decorations.

From 1911 to 1917 Rickenbacker had been a professional racing driver and was known as a daredevil who had won many championships. In 1938 he engineered the purchase of Eastern Air Lines, became its president and held that position until 1953. Thereafter he served as chairman of the company's board until he retired in 1963. During World War II Rickenbacker flew special noncombat missions. On an inspection tour of U. S. air combat groups in 1942, his plane was lost in the Pacific, and he and his crew were given up for dead. But after twenty-one days of brutal exposure on the open sea they were rescued. In his book, *Fighting the Flying Circus,* he tells of his experiences in World War I.

There were, to be sure, some draft dodgers among the German-Americans who kept the American anti-German sentiment aflame. The most publicized case was probably that of the Bergdoll brothers. They were the sons of a prominent brewing family in Philadelphia. Although they were eligible for the draft, they refused to join the army, because "we do not fight our own kind." The brothers became fugitives from the law, and they further added fuel to the anti-German atmosphere by sending taunting postcards to officials of the Justice Department whose agents were for a long time unable to catch them. When the older brother, Erwin, was finally captured, he served half of a four-year sentence in prison. The younger brother, Grover, escaped to Germany at the war's end; but returned later to the United States and had to serve his prison term.

The unstable political situation which developed in Germany during the era of the powerless Weimar Republic was polarized in 1933 between the two hostile camps of the Communists and the National Socialists. Faced with this situation, the majority of German voters chose what they considered

the "lesser evil" and by so doing helped the National Socialists to power. The events which followed led rapidly to
the Second World War. Hitler rejected the Versailles Treaty
in 1935, and in 1936 the German army occupied the demili-
tarized Rhineland.

The military events of World War II are well known, and
it is not necessary to repeat them here. It is worth noting,
however, how many of the outstanding American leaders
were of German stock, such as General Dwight David Eisen-
hower, commander of the Allied forces in Europe; General
Carl Spaatz, who commanded the U.S. bombers in Germany
and Japan; Admiral Chester W. Nimitz, who commanded the
Pacific Fleet; and Generals Eichelberger and Krueger, who
commanded the two armies under General MacArthur in
the Pacific arena.

Part 3

German-Americans in Science and Education

The many stories of the ingenuity and dedication of German-American inventors and scientists are basically the same, and almost seem to repeat themselves over and over again. There have been many of these men who were obsessed with an idea, and brought it to fruition against many hardships and obstacles. I have, therefore, decided to tell you the accomplishments of only a few men of German origin in the fields of science, technology, and education, whose stories will serve to illustrate the contributions of many.

Of the many early engineers of German stock, the Roeblings—father and son—were typical and interesting. John Augustus Roebling, who was to become the most famous bridge builder of the nineteenth century, was born in Muehlhausen, Germany, in 1806. As a high-school student he showed a special talent for geometry and technology. He passed his final examinations in civil engineering at Berlin with high honors, and at the age of twenty he went into the employ of the Prussian government as a surveyor and assistant engineer.

John did not feel too happy in his unchallenging, routine job and emigrated to the United States in 1831 at the invitation of a boyhood friend. He joined a group of German settlers who had bought seven thousand acres of inexpensive, uncultivated land north of Pittsburgh, and started as a pioneer farmer. He married a German girl and named the son born to them Washington Augustus Roebling. Six years of farming were rather unsuccessful for the pioneer family, because John's mind was filled more with improving farm machinery than with farming itself. The archives of the U. S. Patent Office in Washington still preserve a bundle of applications for patents filed by John A. Roebling.

In 1837 Roebling applied for and obtained the position of engineer for the state of Pennsylvania. In this new job Roebling came face to face with the transportation problems created by the Allegheny Mountains. Philadelphia and Pittsburgh were separated by the long ridges of this mountain range. Freight could be shipped through canals to the foot of the mountains, but then had to be hoisted by portage railways to the other side. Boats were placed on cars and pulled over the crest with bulky, expensive hemp ropes. One day John witnessed an accident. A hemp rope broke suddenly and a heavily-loaded railway car rolled backward, killing two workers at the foot of the incline. At this moment John Roebling conceived the idea of constructing a wire rope. He went back to his German farmer friends in Saxonburg and with their help twisted the first crude wire rope in 1841. This new invention helped many industries. Wire rope is used today for logging, quarrying, building skyscrapers and constructing bridges, and for thousands of other purposes.

A new chapter in John Roebling's life began: the building of suspension bridges. His first chance came when, in 1845, the old wooden bridge over the Monongahela River at Pittsburgh was destroyed by fire. The Monongahela Bridge, suspended by wire, took Roebling eight months to build; and it established his reputation among the civil engineers of America. Roebling's next project was the Niagara Bridge, which made him famous all over the world. It was to be a railroad bridge and as such, a novelty, for up till then bridges had been built for men or for horse-drawn vehicles only. Neither the severe Canadian winters nor a cholera epidemic which killed many workers could stop Roebling from finishing his job. It was completed in four years. On March 16, 1855, the first train thundered over the bridge. The Niagara Bridge was suspended from wire cables like the Monongahela, and it became a marvel of the entire world. Visitors came from all parts of the globe wanting to see the famous bridge with their own eyes. The Prince of Wales had his train stopped on the span, so he could walk upon it and take a close look at its construction.

The mighty Ohio River had never been saddled by a bridge at any point. To facilitate commerce between Cincinnati (which had become a great commercial center by 1850) and the state of Kentucky, a bridge over the Ohio River was desirable. A bridge had been planned for more than thirty years; but who could bridge a river a quarter of a mile wide? Roebling said, "It can be done," and in August of 1856 he signed the contract; but it took ten years to finish the project. The depression of 1857 and the Civil War, as well as high waters, floods, and severe winters, delayed the completion of the bridge. When it was opened on December 1, 1866, it was the longest span in the world, measuring 1,057 feet from tower to tower. Exhausted by ten years of all kinds of adversities and saddened by the death of his wife, Roebling had written in his last weeks at Cincinnati, "After this bridge is completed, I shall go home and leave bridge building to younger folks." Yet the Brooklyn Bridge, the culmination of his life's achievements, was still to come.

Brooklyn, by 1865 the fastest growing city of the country, faced New York across the East River. Passengers crossed only by ferryboats. For half a century the cities' fathers had dreamed about a bridge linking New York with Brooklyn. John Roebling, the greatest bridge builder of his time, made this dream come true. He said, "It is no dream at all. We can make it reality." Work on the bridge began in 1869. During reconnaissance for location of the two towers for the bridge, a ferryboat rammed the piles on which Roebling stood, and his foot was caught between two logs and crushed. The doctor amputated all toes of Roebling's right foot; tetanus set in, and on July 22, 1869, John Roebling died.

Roebling's son Washington, who had already assisted his father in building of the Cincinnati Bridge, finished the project. In 1872, Washington Roebling was struck down by "caisson disease," which made him a cripple for the rest of his life. This is the disease divers experience if they come up too suddenly from great depths. Because nitrogen bubbles in the bloodstream do not have time to dissolve, the "bends" or "caisson disease" may result. Through field glasses he was able to supervise the progress of the work from his apartment in Brooklyn. Many of his workers suffered from the same disease, because they had to work in a special type of caisson to lay the foundations of the towers deep under the bed of the river.

Other obstacles had to be conquered: men had to be lured by high wages to work under dangerous conditions and construction costs climbed higher and higher, so that the municipal authorities threatened to stop the project when it was only half-finished. In 1883, after fourteen years of almost superhuman effort, the bridge was opened. It was a day of great celebration: a million spectators came, bands played all day, there was a display of fireworks, and among the first group of dignitaries to cross the bridge were Chester A. Arthur, the president of the United States; Grover Cleveland, the governor of New York; and the mayors of New York and Brooklyn.

The Brooklyn Bridge remained for twenty years the biggest and the most heavily travelled bridge on earth. Today, it is still as sturdy as ever, surviving the test of time. Its two builders are dead but the name of Roebling lives on as one of the greatest in bridge building history.

At the end of World War II a new stream of immigrants entered the United States. More than ten million so-called displaced persons, many of them Germans from Eastern European countries, congregated in West Germany. From there they hoped to be able to establish a new existence overseas. Up to the 1960s about fifty thousand people left Germany yearly. A great number of them found their way to the United States.

Among the newcomers a group of German scientists

under the leadership of Wernher von Braun contributed significantly to the development of aerospace technology in their new homeland. Wernher von Braun was born March 23, 1912, in Posen, a province in the eastern part of Germany. As a confirmation gift he received a telescope from his mother which stimulated his increasing interest in interstellar space flight. At high school his weakest subjects were physics and mathematics, a strange phenomenon for the future Ph.D. in physics. When he found a book filled with mathematical formulae titled *The Rocket to the Interplanetary Spaces* by Hermann Oberth, German pioneer of space flight, he realized that he had to overcome his weakness in mathematics. With determination and will power he became so good in mathematics that he was soon able to tutor his classmates in the subject and even occasionally substituted for the math teacher.

In 1930 he became a student at the Institute of Technology in Berlin, and in the same year joined the Society for Space Travel. Because of limited means and equipment the society literally did not get far off the ground. But in 1932 the German army showed interest in the project and allowed von Braun to use the large army proving ground at Kummersdorf to experiment with liquid fuel rockets. Wernher von Braun made the fateful decision to become a civilian employee of the army because he realized that no private institution could carry out these costly experiments. His own reason for developing the rocket was, in his own words, "Interplanetary travel! Here was a task worth dedicating one's life to. Not just to stare through a telescope at the moon and planets, but to soar through the heavens and actually explore the mysterious universe. I knew how Columbus had felt."[1]

Toward the end of 1934 von Braun and his team launched the first successful twin rockets, which reached an altitude of one and one-half miles. The military was so pleased that they decided to move the rocket team as soon as possible to bigger quarters. Thus in 1937, a new proving ground with a two hundred fifty mile missile range was found near Peenemünde on the Baltic Sea. There work was begun on a rocket which could exceed the range of long-range artillery. After many failures, in October of 1942 a rocket was launched which soared almost sixty miles in height, and about one hundred twenty miles in distance. Adolf Hitler immediately ordered mass production of this new weapon, which was named the V-2 (V stands for *Vergeltungswaffe*, weapon of retribution). It took two more years before the first V-2 was launched to destroy British cities. Wernher von Braun felt sad about this, "We had designed it to blaze the trail to other planets, not to destory our own." He opposed the gestapo who wanted to take over his operation in Peenemünde and who accused von Braun of sabotaging the war effort by directing his effort more to space travel than to the strategic use of his rocket. He was finally imprisoned, and only Hitler's intervention brought about his acquittal at the trial, thus saving his life.

In September of 1944, when the first V-2 was launched, this writer was captured by the Russians. I remember that high-ranking German officers who were captured at that time along with almost the entire German Sixth Army Corps tried to console us by talking about secret weapons which would bring about Germany's final victory. It was an illusion. The V-2, a missile in its infancy, did not prove to be a decisive weapon. In January 1945, Wernher von Braun and his co-workers decided to move to southern Germany, lest they, too, be captured by the Russians. The task was not easy, because it took two trains and about one hundred trucks and cars to transfer the entire rocket operation and its personnel from the Baltic Sea to the Bavarian Alps. But it had to be done, since in von Braun's opinion only the United States with its vast resources was capable of fulfilling his dream of space exploration.

Shortly after Hitler's suicide, Wernher's brother, Magnus von Braun, tried to get in touch with the American army. On April 30, 1945, he surrendered in Reutte, Tyrolia, to the 44th U. S. Infantry Division. The army was not surprised; they had been looking for the German specialists under the code name "Operation Paperclip," instigated by Holger N. Toftoy, chief of the scientific-technological department of the secret service in Paris, who proposed to his superiors to send the rocket specialists as prisoners of war to the United States. The entire rocket team of 127 signed a contract to work under the supervision of Toftoy's department in the United States. The vanguard consisting of Wernher von Braun, Wilhelm Jungert, Erich Neubert, August Schulze, Walter Schwidetzky, Theodor Poppel, and Dr. Eberhard Rees arrived on September 29, 1945, in Fort Strong, Massachusetts. The remaining members of the team arrived in the United States between December 1945 and February 1946, and were sent to Fort Bliss, Texas. The first American V-2 rocket was launched on April 16 from White Sands, New Mexico.

In the meantime, American intelligence hunted for more scientists in Germany and Austria, and a second group of fifty-four specialists arrived in Fort Bliss during 1946. Among these men were three scientists who were to fill important posts two decades later at Cape Kennedy: Dr. Kurt Debus, Dr. Hans Gruene, and Karl Sandler. Early installations were established at Fort Bliss and White Sands, and though these were rather primitive in the beginning, forty-seven V-2 rockets were successfully started before 1952.

By the 1950s the rocket proving grounds were moved to Cape Canaveral (later renamed Cape Kennedy) on the east coast of Florida. When the Russians put their Sputnik into outer space in October 1957, the space race gained momentum. Only four months later, on January 31, 1958, the United States followed by sending *Explorer I* into outer space with the army rocket *Jupiter-C*. The space age had definitely been started and would not be stopped.

Frank Borman, of German descent, belonged to the team of astronauts who, on December 24, 1968, made the first flight around the moon in the *Apollo 8*. On July 20, 1969, *Apollo 11* landed the first man on the moon. That it was an American landing must be attributed to the cooperative efforts of thousands of Americans of all different kinds of ethnic backgrounds, but Wernher von Braun spoke especially for the German scientists who had come with him to America when he said, "It makes me feel that we paid back part of the debt of gratitude we owed our adopted country."[2]

Preceding this group of German rocket specialists were many other noted scientists who had to flee Germany earlier because they were Jews. Martin Schwarzschild left Germany for America in 1937. From 1937 to 1947, he taught astrophysics first at Columbia University and later at Princeton. Biochemist Heinz Fraenkel-Conrat left his hometown of Breslau in 1936 to continue his research at the University of California at Berkeley. Physiologist Otto Meyerhof, who had received the Nobel Prize in 1922, had been in charge of the Kaiser Wilhelm Institute in Berlin from 1921 to 1936. He left Germany in 1938 to become professor of zoology at the University of California.

Foremost among the new immigration of German Jewish scientists was Albert Einstein, father of the theory of relativity. He was born in 1879 at Ulm, and a year later moved with his family to Munich, where his father established a small electrochemical factory. His father was by nature an optimist and quite liberal. Little Albert was sent to a Catholic school and felt at home with the other children. At the age of ten he attended high school and showed an early interest for physics and geometry. He hated Latin and Greek or any schoolwork which had merely to be memorized. But at the age of fourteen he taught himself analytical geometry and differential calculus.

When, in 1894, his father had to sell his factory in Munich and go to Italy, Albert ran away from school and followed his father, because he wanted to study physics and not the classical languages. He persuaded his father to allow him to study at the Polytechnic Institute in Zurich, Switzerland. This institute did not ask for any knowledge of Latin and Greek, but demanded a high school diploma. Einstein had to spend a year at the Swiss high school in Aarau, a town west of Zurich, before he could start his studies at the Polytechnic Institute. He finished his studies in 1900, and since he was not able to find a position as a teacher or as an assistant in a laboratory, he took a job in the Patent Office at Bern, Switzerland. Here he had time to work on his theories, and in 1905 Einstein published his first essay on his new theory, "Electrodynamics of Bodies in Motion." This was soon followed by others which made him famous among European scholars. The University of Zurich made him professor of theoretical physics in 1909. From 1910 to 1912 he taught at the University of Prague. At his return to Zurich he became professor at his alma mater, the Polytechnic Institute.

Max Planck, father of the quantum theory, succeeded in luring Einstein to Berlin in 1913. Planck held Einstein in high regard and called him "the Copernicus of the twentieth century." Einstein became the director of the Kaiser Wilhelm Institute which had been founded by Emperor Wilhelm II solely for research purposes. The Prussian Academy of Sciences made Einstein its honored member. During World War I Einstein was able to continue work on his theories undisturbed. At the age of twenty-two he had become a Swiss citizen and was thus safe from military service in the German army. In the middle of the war Einstein completed his work on the theory of relativity. This theory evoked so much interest that in 1919 Einstein was invited to discuss it all over Europe and even in China and Japan.

Trusting the democratic forces of the Weimar Republic, Einstein became a German citizen again. But he soon became annoyed because his name and his theories were used for political propaganda. In Germany he was called a national hero because he had proven Newton (the pride of England) wrong, while in other European countries his theories were often criticized, not because they were false, but because they had been developed by a German. Nationalism, and with it anti-Semitism, grew steadily in postwar Europe. Einstein was concerned, but, like his father, he was a liberal Jew, and he tried to remain optimistic.

Then in 1932, the Institute for Advanced Study at Princeton offered Einstein a lifetime professorship. He accepted with the understanding that he would spend half of each year in Germany as a member of the Prussian Academy of Sciences, but Hitler's rise to power in January of 1933 made this impossible. Einstein remained at Princeton and became a United States citizen in 1940. In a letter to President Roosevelt, dated August 2, 1939, Einstein pointed out the potential destructive force of an atomic bomb and asked for support to further research in nuclear physics. After World War II, however, Einstein joined the group of scientists who were against the military use of atomic energy. From 1945, he lived in retirement at Princeton and worked on his theories concerning gravitation and electromagnetism. The quantum theory of Planck as well as Einstein's theory of relativity had opened up vast new challenges for physicists. Einstein died in 1955. Winner of the Nobel Prize for physics in 1921, he had remained a modest and unassuming scientist who strove constantly to better the lives of others and who suffered immense grief at the inhumane uses made of some of his discoveries.

Two other seemingly unassuming German-American inventors made news recently, both infringing on the claim of the Wright brothers. Notice of one, Jacob Brodbeck, appeared in the Intelligence Report of the magazine *Parade* October 4, 1975, in a feature titled "Before the Wright Brothers":

> Tomorrow marks the seventieth anniversary of Wilbur and Orville Wright's first flight in a powered airplane. There is substantial evidence, however, that in 1865, thirty-eight years before the Wrights flew their plane at Kitty Hawk, N.C., a German immigrant school teacher, Jacob Brodbeck of Fredericksburg, Texas, invented and flew at treetop level a propeller-driven plane.
>
> Brodbeck, who came from Wittenberg, Germany, taught at the Vereins Kirche (Church) School in Fredericksburg in Lyndon Johnson country.
>
> Brodbeck's biplane had a steering rudder, wings, and a screw propeller powered by springs.
>
> He persuaded the citizens of San Antonio and Gillespie County to buy shares at $1 each to finance a company to manufacture his plane. Unfortunately, his first test flight ended in a crash, and his backers deserted him.
>
> For years Brodbeck toured the United States, seeking new investors. His wife, the former Maria Behrens, and their twelve children, were sure Brodbeck was a mechanical genius, but he could never raise enough capital to prove it. One time while speaking in Michigan, Brodbeck discovered his only set of plane plans had been stolen. He

returned to his farm in Texas, where he died January 8, 1909.

Gustav Weisskopf, the other German-American, suffered equally from lack of funds for his invention. His story appeared as a reprint from a student's paper *Hello, Friends* in the April 1975 edition of the magazine *Solidarity* (page 3), "Wright Brothers Dethroned":

After eight years of painstaking research, the American aviation expert William James O'Dwyer and the writer Miss Stella Randolph established conclusively that the first flight was not the one which the Wright Brothers carried out in 1903, but one made on the 19th of August, 1901, by the German immigrant Gustav Weisskopf. Weisskopf was born in the small Bavarian town of Leutershausen. He learned the trade of a mechanic, but being a restless sort of man, he decided to go to sea.

Eventually, Weisskopf wound up in the United States where he made a certain name for himself as an inventor in the field of construction machinery and railroad brakes. But nothing fascinated him more than the possibility that man might one day be able to take to the air. The obvious next step was to design an air-craft to be propelled by a kerosene engine he built.

The first report about his flight appeared in the Sunday Herald: "Weisskopf flew a single-decker aircraft with a wingspan of thirty-five feet. An acetylene four-stroke engine drove two propellers. Covering half a mile, Weisskopf flew at an altitude of forty to fifty feet over the heads of his friends who had gathered to see the experiment."

After landing, the aviator told the reporter: "I have never before felt as free as during the ten or fifteen minutes I spent airborne. I had a feeling of being way ahead of my brethren because I could fly like a bird."

On the following day, the *New York Herald,* too, reported about the flight.

A second flight over the iced-up Long Island Sound covered a distance of eight miles, but it also cost Weisskopf his flying machine, which was wrecked in the process of landing. This was a blow from which Weisskopf, whose last penny had gone into his aircraft, never recovered.

Apart from the mentioned newspaper reports, the fact that Weisskopf was the first man to fly an engine-driven aircraft is also corroborated by accounts of still living eye-witnesses. And yet, history books and encyclopedias are likely to remain unchanged. This has two reasons: For one thing, it is perfectly correct that the Wright Brothers, while they were not the first ones to fly, had sufficient funds to make the development of aviation a financially viable proposition. They can therefore justifiably be called the fathers of the jet age. But the second reason why Weisskopf will remain forgotten is preposterous: When O'Dwyer presented his findings to Aviation Officials in Washington and asked why Weisskopf is not officially recognized as the first man to have flown an engine-driven aircraft, he was told that this was impossible due to the enormous cost of rewriting history books and encyclopedias.

There is certainly no need for the German-American community to begrudge the fame of the Wright brothers— many more names could be added to the list of German-American inventors and scientists. There were agricultural botanists like Wendelin Grimm, who arrived here from Germany in 1857, bringing with him twenty pounds of alfalfa seed and just enough money to buy a farm in Minnesota. He did not give up planting and experimenting with alfalfa until it became "everlasting clover," something Washington and Jefferson had tried to do on their Virginia plantations but failed. "Minnesota Grimm" as this hardy breed of alfalfa is known today contributed greatly to American farming and ranching.

German-Americans are well represented in the chemical industries: Rosengarten & Sons of Philadelphia, Charles Pfizer & Company of New York, and Sharp & Dohme of Baltimore, to name a few.

Great minds making their mark in any field are not simply born, they must be developed and challenged. A sound educational system brings about such a development and challenge. The impact of German education on the educational system of the United States has been tremendous.

The institutions of family, school, and church were maintained right from the beginning of German settlement in America. During colonial times German communities were settled by farmers and craftsmen who were concerned not only about cutting a living out of the American wilderness, but also saw to it that a church and a schoolhouse were built as soon as possible. Pastorius, the well-educated leader of the first German settlement at Germantown, Pennsylvania, taught not only day school, but also provided night school education for those who had to work during the day or had outgrown the instruction of day school.

Not far from Germantown, in a range of hills known as the Ridge, a group of mystics settled in 1694. Among this group were educated men who contributed to the training of their neighbors' minds. The leader of this brotherhood of the Rosy Cross was John Kelpius. Their founder, John Jacob Zimmerman, a mathematician and astronomer, had died in Rotterdam just before their departure for America. According to Zimmerman's calculations, Christ's triumphal return was to be expected in the fall of 1694.

The brothers built themselves a log house forty feet square, with the sides true to the cardinal points of the compass. One large room served as a meeting place for the brothers; the house also contained small cells for the members and a schoolroom for the children the men gathered and instructed. An observatory was built on top of the sturdy log house where the brethren took turns watching for signs in the sky that announced the coming of the Heavenly Bridegroom.

Not all their time was spent in waiting. Besides instructing the children of adjacent towns and villages, the mystics had various other skills. Some of them possessed medical skills; they planted healing herbs and attended to the sick. As astrologers their advice was sought in casting horoscopes. They also prepared amulets, small pieces of parchment or paper on which magic symbols were inscribed. They were consecrated with occult ceremonies, and were to ward off sickness and evil spirits. The Rosicrucians, as they were called, were considered to be masters of white magic, and their divining rod was called into service by farmers and townspeople to find hidden springs or to indicate the presence of precious metal under the earth's surface.

The Falkner brothers conducted religious services in the Lutheran fashion in the hermitage or in nearby towns. These services were well attended. The brotherhood of the Rosicrucians enjoyed the esteem and sympathy of the other sects to such a degree that Kelpius made an effort to unite the numerous sects into one church. This attempt, however, remained unsuccessful. Mystic healing powers were attributed to Kelpius, and he seemed to have been a kind of religious adviser. In 1708, after fourteen years of waiting for the Heavenly Bridegroom, Kelpius died the death of all Adam's children, although he had hoped to be taken body and soul to his eternal reward. Shortly thereafter, the brotherhood dissolved.

In most instances the German immigrants arrived in family units. Moreover, each family belonged to a religious group of one denomination or the other. It's not difficult to appreciate that these German settlers made every effort to build churches and schools as soon as possible. We mentioned earlier the educational enterprises of Pastorius, Kelpius and his mystics, and those of the United Brethren. But there were more outstanding German schoolteachers in colonial America. One of them was Christopher Dock, the mild-mannered, pious schoolmaster of Montgomery County, Pennsylvania. From 1714 to 1771 he taught the children of Skippack and Salford, alternately, three days a week. He introduced the blackboard into the schoolroom. In 1750 he wrote a book on school teaching which, when printed by Christopher Sauer, became the first pedagogical work published in America. The following excerpts from this book show the author's character and understanding of child psychology:

Dear child, when you come into school incline reverently, sit down quietly in your place, and think of the presence of God. Although after school you are out of the sight of your teacher, God is present in all places; ... Be never idle, never listen at the door. Make your reverence deeply

and lowly with raised face. Never go about nasty and dirty.
If anything is presented to you take it with the right hand
and give thanks courteously. Do not laugh at everything
and especially at the evils and misfortunes of others. If
you have promised anything try to hold to it.[3]

Christopher Dock died as devoutly as he had lived. One
autumn evening, when he did not return home after teaching
school, a search party found him in the schoolhouse on his
knees—dead. Death had overtaken him in his prayers.

Another successful teacher was Thomas Schley. He arrived in 1735 as the leader of about one hundred families
from the Palatinate. They settled in western Maryland and
in 1745 laid out a town named Frederick after the son of
Lord Baltimore. Thomas Schley built the first house in
Frederick's Town. He was in all respects the leader of this
colony. In the absence of a minister he was its preacher and
teacher. Schlatter, pioneer apostle of the Reformed Church,
reports of him,

> It is a great advantage for this congregation that they
> have the best schoolmaster I have met with in America.
> He, Thomas Schley, spares neither labor nor pains in
> instructing the young and edifying the congregation ac-
> cording to his ability, by means of singing and reading the
> word of God, and printed sermons, on every Lord's Day.[4]

Thomas Schley was the ancestor of a long line of men
serving their country well in their day and generation. Jacob
Schley, Thomas's son, became a captain in the Revolutionary
army. A grandson, William Schley, was a member of Congress and governor of Georgia. Other members of the Schley
family became judges and legislators. The most famous
descendant of Thomas Schley, however, was Admiral Winfield Scott Schley, who in 1898 destroyed the Spanish fleet
under Admiral Cervera at Santiago, Cuba.

John Ulmer, the schoolmaster of Broad Bay, Massachusetts, was a man of many talents. When its minister left the
hardpressed settlement, Ulmer filled his place by holding
religious services in barns, since the government had not

kept its promise to provide means for the building of a church. During the Spanish War he led a contingent of German soldiers in the siege of Louisburg on Cape Brenton.

The bond between "family, school, and church" was indeed very dear to the early German settlers (sectarians as well as church people), as the following statement, published in 1755 in Pennsylvania, may indicate: "The Germans have schools and meetinghouses in almost every township thro' the province, and have more churches and other places of worship in the city of Philadelphia itself than those of all other persuasions added together."[5]

Up to 1820 American education had been largely influenced first by British and then by French systems. The War of 1812 with Britain and the defeat of Napoleon at Waterloo in 1815 cooled U.S. relations with the two countries. Madame de Stael's famous book on Germany was translated into English in 1814, and statements in it such as the following made American educators look to Germany for inspiration: "All the north of Germany is filled with the most learned universities in Europe. In no country, not even in England, have the people so many means of instructing themselves, and of bringing their faculties to perfection—the literary glory of Germany depends altogether upon these institutions."[6]

It has been estimated that before 1900 approximately ten thousand Americans were educated at German universities. Among those ten thousand American students were quite a few future luminaries of United States' educational philosophy. It is only natural that the educational experience gained in Germany by such men as George Ticknor, George Bancroft, Joseph Green Cogswell, Ralph Waldo Emerson, Henry Wadsworth Longfellow, and others affected the American universities at which they later taught. The great universities in the East looked to German universities for advice in developing their graduate schools. Daniel C. Gilman, first president of Johns Hopkins, declared, "As Latin was the language of the scholar during the Middle Ages, so the knowledge of German is indispensable now for anyone who claims the name of a student and scholar."[7]

At the twenty-fifth anniversary celebration of the Johns Hopkins University in 1902, President Eliot of Harvard addressed the retiring president of Johns Hopkins as follows:

> President Gilman, your first achievement here, with the help of your colleagues, your students, and your trustees, has been, to my thinking—and I have had good means of observation—the creation of a school of graduate studies, which has lifted every other university in the country in its departments of arts and sciences. I want to testify that the graduate school of Harvard University, started feebly in 1870 and 1871, did not thrive until the example of Johns Hopkins forced our faculty to put their strength into the development of our instruction for graduates. And what was true of Harvard was true of every other university in the land which aspired to create an advanced school of arts and sciences.[8]

Madame de Stael's book on Germany indirectly influenced the educational philosophy and direction of Eastern universities. The report on the Prussian school system by the Frenchman, M. Victor Cousin, its English translation republished in 1835 in the United States, became the standard of imitation for universities in the Midwest. This was especially true for the University of Michigan founded in 1837. Calvin Thomas described the event as follows:

> A university in the German sense—an institution crowning the education system of a state, treating its students as adults engaged in a bona fide pursuit of knowledge, offering its advantages at the lowest possible prices, sending down its roots into the life of the people, to take then the sap of its own vitality, and paying back the debt by raising the intelligence and adding to the value and dignity of life through the entire commonwealth—a university upon this theory was an experiment yet to be tried. That the experiment came to be tried in Michigan, under reasonably favorable conditions, is largely due to Mr. Pierce, whose office was modeled after that of the Prussian Minister of Public Instruction, and who is said to have been the first American to hold such a position under state government.[9]

The same principle was applied in the founding of the University of Wisconsin. And it seems to be no mere coincidence that the best expression of gratitude by an American university to German educational influences was given on March 22, 1904, at the Fiftieth Convocation of the University of Chicago in its "Recognition of the Indebtedness of American Universities to the Ideals of German Scholarship."

In 1837 the reform of the American public school system on the elementary and secondary level was primarily the work of Horace Mann. His reforms were largely influenced by his visit to Germany and his survey of German schools. It would be foolish, however, to assert that the American school system is a mere *abklatsch* of European school systems. With all due respect to the British, French, and German influences, American education came well into its own. It is even possible that today the European schools on all levels may profitably look at American schools for inspiration and rejuvenation.

In addition, there were two unique German contributions to American education. The influence of the German *Turner* or gymnasts on the physical education of American boys and girls was mentioned in a previous chapter. The first kindergarten in America was founded by Margarethe Meyer-Schurz. The kindergarten is based on the pedagogical principles of Friedrich Froebel. Late in his life, Froebel lectured in Hamburg, the hometown of Margarethe Meyer-Schurz, where he found an enthusiastic listener in the then sixteen-year-old girl. Later Margarethe helped her sister to establish the first kindergarten in England. Her sister's husband Johannes Ronge and her brother Adolf Meyer had to leave Germany for England because of their liberal ideas. In England they became the pioneers of Froebel's educational philosophy. Margarethe met Carl Schurz at her brother-in-law's home. It was love at first sight, and they were married in London July 6, 1852.

In the autumn of 1856 the Schurzes settled with their three-year-old daughter Agathe in Watertown, Wisconsin. Margarethe gathered the children of relatives and friends in the house of her parents-in-law, which was conveniently located in downtown Watertown. Here the children played with little Agathe under Margarethe's supervision; the first American kindergarten was born. The kindergarten movement gained momentum when Mrs. Schurz made the acquaintance of Elizabeth Peabody in 1859 in Boston. In 1867 Ms. Peabody went to Germany to study the idea of the kindergarten at its source. From then on she devoted her entire life to the propagation of the kindergarten. Today, almost every elementary school in the United States has at least one spacious, friendly, sunny room for a kindergarten, the word meaning, literally, "a garden of or for children."

To conclude this survey of German-American contributions to education in the United States, it should be noted that many colleges, including Oberlin, Heidelberg, and Wittenberg, were founded by German-American groups. These small colleges continue to provide education in the liberal arts and sciences and are well known for their schools of music, education, and science today.

The history of Germans in America is an honorable one. This book touches on some of the highlights of German contributions to the rise of this great nation. To be sure, I have not written all that could have been said. Nevertheless, I hope to have helped to bring about better understanding of the role of German-Americans in our history. Speaking, I am sure, for many German-Americans, I can say that we are proud to be American citizens, and at the same time, proud to be of German origin.

Notes

PART 1—GERMAN-AMERICANS IN AMERICAN LIFE

1. Albert B. Faust, *The German Element in the United States,* 2 vols. (Boston and New York: Houghton Mifflin Co., 1909), vol. 1, p. 285.
2. Friedrich Muench settled as a farmer in Warren County, Missouri, in 1834.
3. Gottfried Duden spent four years, 1824 to 1828, in Missouri as a gentleman farmer. After his return to Germany, he wrote an idyllic account of his stay in Missouri, combining fact and fiction.
4. Friedrich Hecker, German-American idol during the Civil War. He settled in Belleville, Illinois, in 1849.
5. Faust, *The German Element,* vol. 1, pp. 588–89.

Chapter 2—The Early Communities

1. Lucy Forney Bittinger, *The Germans in Colonial Times* (First published, 1901; reprinted, New York: Russell & Russell, 1968), p. 32.
2. Ibid., p. 158.
3. Ibid., p. 170.
4. Faust, *The German Element,* vol. 1, p. 136.

5. Bittinger, *Germans in Colonial Times,* p. 83.
6. Ibid., p. 83.
7. Faust, *The German Element,* vol. 1, p. 159.
8. Ibid., vol. 1, p. 160.
9. Ibid., vol. 1, pp. 160–61.
10. Ibid., vol. 1, p. 172.
11. Ibid., vol. 1, p. 181.
12. Ibid., vol. 1, p. 199.
13. Grace Kelley, Casey Stengel, and Louis H. Sullivan are famous offspring of German-Irish marriages.
14. Gotthardt Dellmann Bernheim, *History of the German settlements and of the Lutheran Church in North and South Carolina* (The Lutheran Bookstore, Philadelphia, 1872), p. 148.
15. Bittinger, *Germans in Colonial Times,* p. 182.
16. Ibid., p. 182.
17. Ibid., pp. 121–22.
18. Faust, *The German Element,* vol. 1, pp. 216–17.
19. Ibid., vol. 1, p. 236.
20. Ibid., vol. 1, p. 241.

Chapter 3—The Near West

1. Theodore Roosevelt, *The Winning of the West,* vol. 1 (New York: G. P. Putnam's Sons, 1895), pp. 145–46.
2. Faust, *The German Element,* vol. 1, p. 430.
3. Ibid., vol. 1, pp. 430–31.

Chapter 4—The Middle-West

1. Gottfried Duden, *Bericht ueber eine Reise nach den westlichen Staaten Nordamerikas* (Elberfeld: Sam. Lucas, 1829), p. 73.
2. Faust, *The German Element,* vol. 1, p. 443.
3. Richard O'Connor, *The German-Americans* (Boston: Little, Brown & Co., 1968), p. 81.
4. John Arkas Hawgood, *The Tragedy of German-America* (New York: Arno Press, 1970), p. 113.
5. Ibid., pp. 113–14.
6. Samuel F. Harrison, *History of Hermann, Missouri* (Chicago: Goodspeed Publ. Co., 1966), quotation on back cover.
7. Hawgood, *Tragedy of German-America,* p. 122.

8. Ibid., p. 123.
9. O'Connor, *German-Americans,* p. 83.
10. Marguerite Young, *Angel in the Forest* (New York: Charles Scribner's Sons, 1945), pp. 22-23.
11. O'Connor, *German-Americans,* p. 223.
12. Anton Eickhoff, *In der neuen Heimath* (New York: E. Steiger & Co., 1884), pp. 376-77.
13. Faust, *The German Element,* vol. 1, pp. 464-65.

Chapter 6—The South-West: Texas

1. Hawgood, *Tragedy of German-America,* pp. 154-55.

Chapter 7—The Far West

1. Victor W. von Hagen, *Der Ruf der Neuen Welt* (Muenchen, Zurich: Droemer Knaur, 1970), p. 272 (my translation).
2. A more detailed account of the life-work of some of these men will be given in the following chapter.

Chapter 8—German-Americans in Business and Sports

1. Faust, *The German Element,* vol. 2, p. 139.
2. O'Connor, *German-Americans,* p. 367.
3. This section on baseball is an adaptation of Richard O'Connor's chapter, "An Aptitude for Baseball," in *German Americans,* pp. 309-13. All quotations are used as in that chapter.

Chapter 9—The Forty-Eighters and the Turner Societies

1. O'Connor, *German-Americans,* p. 122.
2. Lawrence S. Thompson, Frank X. Braun, "The Forty-Eighters in Politics," Adolf Edward Zucker, editor, *The Forty-Eighters: Political Refugees of the Revolution of 1848* (New York: Columbia University Press, 1950; reprinted, New York: Russell & Russell, 1967), p. 121. This and all other quotations from this book reprinted by permission of Columbia University Press.
3. O'Connor, *German-Americans,* p. 128.
4. Zucker, *Forty-Eighters,* p. 127.
5. O'Connor, *German-Americans,* p. 128.

6. F. I. Herriot, "The Germans of Chicago and Stephen A. Douglas," *Deutsch Amerikanische Geschichtsblaetter,* 12 (1913), p. 250.
7. Zucker, *Forty-Eighters,* pp. 132-33.
8. Faust, *The German Element,* vol. 2, pp. 183-84.
9. Ibid.
10. Hildegard Binder Johnson, "Adjustment to the United States," in Zucker, *Forty-Eighters,* pp. 67-68.
11. Eitel W. Dobert, "The Radicals," in Zucker, *Forty-Eighters,* p. 173.
12. Ibid., p. 169.
13. Arthur C. Cole, *The Era of the Civil War* (n.p.: McClung, 1922), p. 215.
14. Zucker, *Forty-Eighters,* p. 96.
15. Ibid., p. 100.

Chapter 10—Carl Schurz and Franz Lieber

1. Carl Schurz, *The Reminiscence of Carl Schurz,* 3 vols. (New York: The McClure Co., 1907), vol. 1, pp. 399–400.
2. Bayard Quincy Morgan, "Carl Schurz," in Zucker, *Forty-Eighters,* pp. 229-30.
3. O'Connor, *German-Americans,* p. 164.
4. Ibid., pp. 165-66.
5. Zucker, *Forty-Eighters,* p. 236.
6. Schurz, *Reminiscences,* vol. 3, p. 302.
7. Zucker, *Forty-Eighters,* p. 245.
8. O'Connor, *German-Americans,* p. 178.
9. Zucker, *Forty-Eighters,* pp. 249-50.
10. Ibid., p. 240.
11. Hawgood, *Tragedy of German-America,* p. 285.

Chapter 11—Political Activism

1. O'Connor, *German-Americans,* p. 278.
2. Ibid., p. 277.
3. Marvin and Bernard Kalb, *Kissinger* (Boston: Little, Brown & Co., 1974), illustration 9.

Chapter 12—Musical Traditions

1. Faust, *The German Element,* vol. 2, p. 256.

2. Ibid., p. 260.
3. O'Connor, *German-Americans,* pp. 418-19.
4. Ibid., p. 420.
5. Ibid., p. 421.

Chapter 13—Printing and Publishing

1. O'Connor, *German-Americans,* p. 282.

Chapter 14—German Food and Drink

1. Herman Hagedorn, *The Hyphenated Family* (New York: Macmillan, 1960), p. 85.
2. John F. Kennedy, *A Nation of Immigrants* (New York: Harper & Row, 1964), p. 53.

Chapter 15—Social and Labor Reform

1. Carl Wittke, *We Who Built America* (New York: Prentice Hall, Inc., 1939), pp. 239-40.
2. Eitel W. Dobert, "The Radicals," in Zucker, *Forty-Eighters,* p. 180.
3. Wittke, *We Who Built America,* pp. 240-41.
4. Faust, *The German Element,* vol. 2, pp. 196-97.

PART 2—GERMAN-AMERICANS IN U.S. MILITARY HISTORY

Chapter 16—The Frontier Wars

1. Bittinger, *Germans in Colonial Times,* pp. 187-88.
2. Ibid., p. 188.
3. Ibid., p. 189.
4. Ibid., pp. 189-90.
5. Ibid., pp. 191-92.
6. Ibid., p. 196.
7. Ibid., p. 197.
8. Ibid., p. 197.
9. Ibid., p. 197.
10. Ibid., p. 199.

11. Ibid., p. 199.
12. Ibid., pp. 192-93.
13. Ibid., p. 194.
14. Faust, *The German Element*, vol. 1, pp. 278-80.

Chapter 17—The German-Americans during the War of Independence

1. Rufus W. Griswold, *The Republican Court: or American Society in the Days of Washington* (New York: D. Appleton Co., 1856), pp. 153-54.
2. Faust, *The German Element*, vol. 1, p. 338.
3. Bittinger, *Germans in Colonial Times*, p. 260.
4. Faust, *The German Element*, vol. 1, p. 308.
5. Ibid., p. 308.
6. O'Connor, *German-Americans*, p. 46.
7. Ibid., p. 47.
8. Ibid., p. 48.
9. John M. Palmer, *General von Steuben* (Port Washington, N.Y.: Kennikat Press Inc., 1937), p. 157.
10. Faust, *The German Element*, vol. 1, p. 324.
11. Ibid., p. 327.
12. Ibid., p. 329.
13. Ibid., p. 329.
14. Ibid., pp. 329-30.
15. O'Connor, *German-Americans*, p. 37.
16. Faust, *The German Element*, vol. 1, p. 303.
17. Ibid., pp. 303-04.
18. O'Connor, *German-Americans*, p. 44.
19. Faust, *The German Element*, vol. 1, pp. 343-44.
20. Bittinger, *Germans in Colonial Times*, p. 282.

Chapter 18—The War of 1812

1. Faust, *The German Element*, vol. 1, p. 515, footnote 1.
2. *Jaeger* means, literally, "hunter"; here it means "cavalry."

Chapter 20—The Civil War

1. Faust, *The German Element*, vol. 1, p. 533.
2. Free translation by the crowd of the name of one of the German regiments, *Die schwarze Garde*.

3. Augustus J. Prahl, "The Turner," in Zucker, *Forty-Eighters,* p. 105.
4. Ella Lonn, "The Forty-Eighters in the Civil War," in Zucker, *Forty-Eighters,* p. 184.
5. Ibid., p. 190.
6. Ibid., p. 190.
7. Ibid., p. 192.
8. Lew Wallace, *An Autobiography,* 2 vols. (New York: Harper & Brothers, 1906), vol. 2, pp. 560-62.
9. Faust, *The German Element,* vol. 1, p. 549.
10. Ibid., p. 551.
11. Ibid., p. 566.

Chapter 22—World Wars I and II

1. Walter Millis, *The Road to War: America 1914-1917* (Boston: Houghton Mifflin Co., 1935), p. 72.
2. O'Connor, *German-Americans,* p. 410.
3. Ibid., pp. 410-11.
4. Ibid., p. 29.
5. Ibid., p. 423.
6. Ibid., pp. 426-27.

PART 3—GERMAN-AMERICANS IN SCIENCE AND EDUCATION

1. Dieter Cunz, *They Came from Germany* (New York: Dodd, Mead & Co., 1966), p. 139–40.
2. Ibid., p. 157.
3. Bittinger, *Germans in Colonial Times,* pp. 112-13.
4. Faust, The German Element, vol. 1, pp. 169-70.
5. Rudolf Cronau, *Drei Jahrhunderte deutschen Lebens in Amerika* (Berlin: Dietrich Reimer [Ernst Vohsen], 1909), p. 151.
6. Faust, *The German Element,* vol. 2, p. 210.
7. O'Connor, *German-Americans,* p. 274.
8. Faust, *The German Element,* vol. 2, pp. 229-30.
9. Ibid., pp. 220-21.

Bibliography

Bernheim, Rev. Gotthardt Dellmann. *History of the German Settlements and the Lutheran Church in North and South Carolina.* Philadelphia: The Lutheran Bookstore, 1872.

Bittinger, Lucy Forney. *The Germans in Colonial Times.* (First published, 1901; reprinted, New York: Russell & Russell, 1968.)

Cole, Arthur C. *The Era of the Civil War.* McClung, 1922.

Collins, L. *Historical Sketches of Kentucky.* 1847.

Cronau, Rudolf. *Drei Jahrhunderte Deutchen Lebens in Amerika.* Berlin: Dietrich Reimer (Ernst Vohsen), 1909.

Cunz, Dieter. *They Came from Germany.* New York: Dodd, Mead & Co., 1966.

Das Buch der Deutschen in Amerika, edited under the auspices of the National German American Alliance, Walther's Printing Shop, Philadelphia, 1909.

Dictionary of American Biography, 21 vols., ed. by Allen Johnson and Dumas Malone. New York: Charles Scribner's Sons, 1928-1944.

Duden, Gottfried. *Bericht Ueber Eine Reise Nach den Westliche Staaten Nordamerikas.* Elberfeld: Sam. Lucas, 1829.

Eickhoff, Anton. *In der Neuen Heimat.* New York: E. Steiger & Co., 1884.

Faust, Albert Bernhardt. *The German Element in the United States with Special Reference to Its Political, Moral, Social, and Educational Influence,* 2 vols. Boston and New York: Houghton Mifflin Co., 1909.

Gould, B. A. *Investigations in the Military and Anthropological Statistics of American Soldiers.* New York, 1869.

Griswold, Rufus W. *The Republican Court: or American Society in the Days of Washington.* New York: D. Appleton Co., 1856.

Hagedorn, Herman. *The Hyphenated Family.* New York: Mac-Millan Co., 1960.

Harrison, Samuel F. *History of Hermann, Missouri.* Chicago: Goodspeed Publishing Co., 1966.

Hawgood, John Arcas. *The Tragedy of German-America.* New York: Arno Press, 1970.

Herriot, F. I. "The Germans of Chicago and Stephen A. Douglas, *Deutsch Amerikanische Geschichtsblaetter,* 12 (1913).

Kalb, Marvin, and Kalb, Bernard. *Kissinger.* Boston: Little, Brown & Co., 1974.

Kennedy, John F. *A Nation of Immigrants.* New York: Harper & Row, 1964.

Millis, Walter. *The Road to War: America 1914-1917.* Boston: Houghton Mifflin Co., 1935.

O'Connor, Richard. *The German-Americans.* Boston: Little, Brown & Co., 1968.

Palmer, John M. *General von Steuben.* Port Washington, N. Y.: Kennikat Press Inc., 1937.

Parade Magazine, July 14, 1974, and October 4, 1975.

Roosevelt, Theodore. *The Winning of the West,* 4 vols. New York: G. P. Putnam's Sons, 1895.

Schurz, Cal. *The Reminiscences of Carl Schurz,* 3 vols. New York: McClure Co., 1907.

Solidarity (Official organ of the Workmen's Benefit Fund of the United States), vol. 69, no. 4, April, 1975.

Thwaites, Reuben G. "Preliminary Notes on the Distribution of Foreign Groups in Wisconsin." Extract from *Annual Report,* Wisconsin Hist. Soc., 1890.

Von Hagen, Victor W. *Der Ruf der Neuen Welt.* Muenchen and Zuerich: Droemer Knaur, 1970.

Wallace, Lew. *An Autobiography,* 2 vols. New York and Boston: Harper & Brothers, 1906.

Wittke, Carl. *We Who Built America.* New York: Prentice-Hall Inc., 1939.

Young, Marguerite. *Angel in the Forest.* New York: Charles Scribner's Sons, 1945.

Zucker, Adolf Edward, ed. *The Forty-Eighters: Political Refugees of the Revolution of 1848* (New York: Columbia University Press, 1950; reprinted, New York: Russell & Russell, 1967).

Index

Schumann, George Washington, 119
Schumann, Paul, 119
Schumann-Keink, Ernestine, 118–20
Schurz, Agathe, 210–11
Schurz, Carl, 87, 88, 95–106, 173, 177–78, 210
Schurz, Margarethe Meyer, 96
Schwab, Michael, 133, 186
Schwan, Theodor, 184
Schwarzendorf, Johann, 129
Schwarzschild, Martin, 200
Schwidetzsky, Walter, 199
Science, 197–204
Scott, Winfield, 172
Seattle, Wash., 64–65
Seidl, Anton, 117
Semple, Letitia Tyler, 170
Settlement, patterns of, 12–32
Seward, William H., 97, 98
Sharp and Dohme (Baltimore), 204
Sharpburg, Md., 24
Shearer, Lloyd, 112
Sherman, William T., 178
Shirley, William, 30, 138
Sicilian War of Liberation, 110
Sigel, Franz, 98, 173, 176–77
Sink (Zink), Rev., 36
Six Nations, 139–40
Slavery, 13, 46
Smith, John, quoted, 10–11
Smith, Rev., 36
Smith, William, 15
Socialism, 130–31, 132
Socialist party, 132
Social reform, 130–34
Solidarity, 203
Sonoma Valley, Calif., 65
Sound Money League of Pennsylvania, 73
South Carolina, 28–29
South Carolina College, 108
Spaatz, Carl, 191
Spangerberg, August Gottlieb, 27, 140; quoted, 16
Spanish American War, 183–84
Speyer, Germany, 30, 74
Spies, August, 132
Spiritual Magazine, 123

Sports, 76–80
Spotswood, Alexander, 24
Spreckels, Claus, 66, 71–72
Spreckels' building (San Francisco), 72
Sputnik I, 199
Squibb, Edward Robinson, 112
Staatsanzeiger (Ill.), 85
Stael, Madame de, 209
"Star-Spangled Banner," 170
Steiger, Andrew, 22
Steiger's Meadow, 22
Steinmetz, Charles, 75–76
Steinway, Henry, 120
Steinway, Theodore, 120
Steinway & Sons, 120
Steinwehr, Adolf von, 173, 180–81
Sternberg, George M., 184
Steuben, Baron von, 153–56
Steuben Society, 156
Steuben's Regulations (Blue Book), 155
Steubenville, Ohio, 37
Stirk, John, 162
Stirling, Lord, 149
Stoner, Michael, 34
Stockton Mining Co., 66
Stone Arabia, Mohawk Valley, 21
Story, Joseph, 107
Stovall, George, 79
Strader, George, 33
Stricker, John, 169–70
Struve, Gustav, 132
Stuart, Jeb, 182
Sugar industry, 71–72
Sullivan County, Tenn., 36
Sumner, Charles, 107
Sunday observance controversy, 92
Sutter, John August, 70–71
Swann, Thomas, 93

Talbot, Gov., quoted, 10
Taneytown, Md., 24
Taylor, Zachary, 171
Technology, 193–96
Tennessee, 36
Tennessee Synod, 37
Tesla, Nikola, quoted, 75
Texas, 59–62
Thayendanegea, 151